BLUE STREAK

BLUE STREAK

Swearing, Free Speech, and Sexual Harassment

RICHARD DOOLING

 RANDOM HOUSE   NEW YORK

Grateful acknowledgment is made to the following for permission to reprint previously published material:

FARRAR, STRAUS & GIROUX, INC.: Excerpt from "Revelation" from *The Complete Stories* by Flannery O'Connor. Copyright © 1971 by the Estate of Mary Flannery O'Connor. Excerpts from "Introduction to a Memoir of Mary Ann" from *Mystery and Manners* by Flannery O'Connor, edited by Sally Fitzgerald. Copyright © 1969 by the Estate of Mary Flannery O'Connor. Excerpts from the Foreword by John Freccero from *The Inferno of Dante: A New Verse Translation* by Robert Pinsky. Foreword copyright © 1994 by John Freccero. Reprinted by permission of Farrar, Straus & Giroux, Inc.

The International Journal of Psycho-Analysis AND LEO STONE, M.D.: Excerpt from "On the Principal Obscene Word in the English Language" by Leo Stone, M.D. (*The International Journal of Psycho-Analysis*, Vol. XXXV, 1954, pages 30–54). Copyright © 1954 by The International Journal of Psycho-Analysis. Reprinted by permission of *The International Journal of Psycho-Analysis* and Leo Stone, M.D.

Newsweek: Excerpt from "Is the Mind an Illusion?" (*Newsweek*, April 20, 1992). Copyright © 1992 by Newsweek, Inc. Reprinted by permission of *Newsweek.*

The Ohio State Journal of Law AND KINGSLEY R. BROWNE: Excerpt from "Title VII as Censorship: Hostile Environment Harassment and the First Amendment" by Kingsley R. Browne (*The Ohio State Journal of Law*, Vol. 52, 1991, pages 481–550). Copyright © 1991 by Kingsley R. Browne. Reprinted by permission of *The Ohio State Journal of Law* and Kingsley R. Browne, Wayne State University Law School, Detroit, MI.

Salmagundi: Excerpt from "The Metamorphosis of Shit" by Martin Pops (*Salmagundi*, Vol. 56, 1982, pages 26–61). Reprinted by permission of *Salmagundi.*

WASHINGTON UNIVERSITY: Excerpt from "Learning to Talk" by William Gass (*Washington University Magazine*, Spring 1979). Reprinted courtesy of *Washington University Magazine*, Washington University in St. Louis.

Library of Congress Cataloging-in-Publication Data

Dooling, Richard.
    Blue streak: swearing, free speech, and sexual harassment /
    Richard Dooling.—1st ed.
        p. cm.
    ISBN 0-679-44471-8
    1. Swearing. 2. Swearing—Psychological aspects. 3. Men—Psychology.
I. Title.
GT3080.D66 1996
394—dc20 95-26083

Random House website address: http://www.randomhouse.com/

Printed in the United States of America on acid-free paper

9 8 7 6 5 4 3 2

First Edition

For Bill & Diane,
and for big brother Bob

Acknowledgments

I wish to thank Harold Evans for his enthusiastic support. I also wish to thank my editor, Daniel Menaker, for giving away so many good ideas.

Contents

BLUE STREAK

Why Men Swear More Than Women

When a gentleman is disposed to swear, it is not for any standers-by to curtail his oaths.

—Shakespeare, *Cymbeline*, act II, scene I

Men and women can be very different—an observation that was once so self-evident nobody could make a dime writing about it. Nowadays, it's front-page news and the stuff of how-to best-sellers when brain scientists or social psychologists tell us that there are "real" differences in the ways men and women think, communicate, or behave. "No, really," the authors seem to be telling us, "studies have shown that ring-tailed lemurs and Alaskan king crabs are different."

I thought it might be safe to observe that, generally speaking, men swear more than women. But these days even the most innocent generalization can earn you public infamy and several lawsuits, so I went to the bookstore to see if this difference had been addressed in Deborah Tannen's *You Just Don't Understand* (which I'm told is about how men and women communicate differently) and *Talking from 9 to 5* (which I'm told is about how men and women communicate differently during working hours), and John Gray's *Men Are from Mars, Women Are from Venus.*

Zip. I was amazed to find nothing about the male proclivity for swearing, and no entries in the indices under "c" for curse or cuss, "p" for profanity, or "s" for swear (nothing under "f" either). How can books purporting to analyze communication differences between the sexes fail to observe that men swear and use the f-word oftener than they say hello, and that women generally swear much less often, and almost never use the f-word? I tried to read *You Just Don't Understand* and was instantly reminded of *I'm OK, You're OK,* recast to accommodate the incessant noise and transactional analysis of gender politics. Even the title tells you it's definitely not a guy book, because it sounds like a line of dialogue from the last argument you had with your girlfriend.

"I wish you wouldn't swear so much," she says.

"Why?" you innocently protest.

"You just don't understand," she says. "Words can hurt."

"Oh really?" you say. "Show me sometime, because I don't believe it."

If you do a Humphrey or a Marlon on her, she might publicly accuse you of insensitivity. Don't use the old sticks-and-stones cliché. Be cultivated. Brush up your Shakespeare, make a contemplative moue, and tell her:

Why Men Swear More Than Women

But words are words. I never yet did hear
That the bruised heart was pierced through the ear.

But Bill is dead, was white and male, and has become a pillar of Western Civilization (a smear in this day and age), so she may prefer the Arabic proverb "A thousand curses never tore a shirt." (Lie and tell her a redoubtable Persian warlady of color made it up.)

Men swear because we are uncouth warthogs by nature, and we especially love to say bad words, because it makes us feel manly in some violent, disturbing way, which (government-funded studies will someday show) is indicative of the male need to exploit, debase, and discriminate against women. Tempting litigation, may I suggest that men and women react differently to swearing? A male "harassed" by someone using foul language in the workplace will typically turn to his harasser and forthrightly advise him to fuck himself and keep the baby. A litigious feminist in similar circumstances will be more apt to file a formal complaint with the Equal Employment Opportunity Commission (EEOC), and then look forward with great anticipation to the day she will be allowed to take the stand and testify in careful detail about all the ignominy and injustice she has suffered in the workplace.

Yes, you can be sued if you cuss a lot, especially if you are a male employer and you swear liberally in the workplace, and a court later determines that you created an oppressive or hostile environment—a species of sexual harassment under the geometrically expanding reach of

Title VII—a federal statute that originally banned discrimination in employment and is now being read to ban "ridicule," "insult," and sexual innuendo as well. There are reported cases of men who sued their employers because they believed their employers' foul language created a sexually hostile work environment, but most of those guys can't be reached for comment, or else they had enough sense to use John Does. More to the point, they lost, because they weren't women.

In the name of civil rights and in response to gender politics, the government now intrudes into almost every important aspect of our occupational lives. If you want to say, "Girls, let's get butt-naked and fuck!" you better be a rap musician, like Ice-T (who in fact penned just that precious sentiment), or a member of 2 Live Crew, which sells to teenagers millions of compact discs containing songs called "The Fuck Shop," "Me So Horny," and "Dick Almighty." If you are a Hollywood actor, like Arnold or Bruce, you can scream, "FUCK YOU, MOTHERFUCKER!" while spraying hollow-point bullets and opening holes in Arab terrorists big enough to admit shafts of sunlight. But if you are a regular male working stiff, once you punch the clock at work you can be sued for sexual harassment and fired if you fail to use "foreperson" instead of "foreman," or for saying, "Wow, Wilma, that dress you're wearing really sets off your figure."

We are currently on a cusp of taboos, where formerly prohibited terms for sex and excrement are becoming much more acceptable and are being replaced by the new unspeakables: racial or ethnic slurs and gender stereotypes. If you think this is still a free country where—as long as you don't physically harm your fellow citizens—you can pretty much say and do whatever you please, try this experiment. The next time you are forced to attend one of those sensitivity training sessions at work, wait until the gender-equity specialist (who makes more than you do, and does it by talking) asks you to say a little something about yourself and how you feel about sensitivity training. Take that Pall Mall straight from behind your ear, and fire it up. Pull your *Playboy* out of its brown paper, and set it next to your copy of *Guns & Ammo*. Then fetch out your hip flask, and draw off a shot of Jim Beam neat. Exhale that first immensely satisfying puff, pucker up to a sip of old Jim, and say, "Honey, what's all that racket comin' out your mouth? Why, it sounds like two skeletons fuckin' on a footlocker!"

Not everyone appreciates the restorative powers of bluestreak cussing and a good mouth-filling oath. And it takes a mental heavyweight like Nietzsche to appreciate the profound efficacy of rudeness:

> It also seems to me that the rudest word, the rudest letter are still more benign, more decent than silence. Those who remain silent are almost always lacking in delicacy and courtesy of the heart. Silence is an objection; swallowing things leads of necessity to a bad character—it even upsets the stomach. All who remain silent are dyspeptic. [*Ecce Homo*, as translated by Walter Kaufman]

Swearing achieves the same catharsis one gets from a hearty belch, an evening constitutional, or a good, long cry—it's a psychic purgative when one is suffering from emotional constipation. Because men are congenitally incapable of indulging in good, long cries, swearing provides them with a handy compromise when presented with the impractical alternatives of running away, crying, or fighting. Men can be hostile creatures, and swearing often allows them to exchange oaths instead of blows. As Mark Twain put it in *Pudd'nhead Wilson,* "When angry, count four; when very angry, swear."

Instead of the apes at the water hole in *2001: A Space Odyssey,* take the example of ten men playing a competitive, pickup game of basketball. A talentless stiff throws up a shot that has no hope of seeing backboard, rim, or net, and then unjustifiably calls a foul on you for nothing more than a bit of incidental contact. What do you do?

Normally, blows are out of the question, if for no other reasons than the high insurance deductibles, the long waits, and the family members of gunshot victims one encounters during emergency room visits. But *something* needs to be done, because the guy who called the foul happens to be a fucking pussy who routinely calls fouls to compensate for his inability to take it to the hoop. He has been watching more sports from the couch than he's been playing on the court, has nourished a swag-bellied paunch, and has turned into a fat-ass, paper-pushing pussy. So, instead of hitting him, you say: "Foul, my fucking ass! Find the keys to the ladies' room and go pee sitting down!

Only the Pillsbury Doughboy would call *that* a fucking foul!"

Most likely the offender will formulate a passable rejoinder, featuring as many fuck-yous as possible and ending with a reciprocal attack on your masculinity. You'll give him the ball back at the top of the key, along with a verbal prescription for some Midol, and all will be forgotten . . . until he calls another one.

That swearing is primarily a male avocation may help explain why many of the examples of usage given for the f-word in the new dictionaries of slang come from the military and its peacekeeping efforts abroad. A 1921 citation from *Notes & Queries,* referring to World War I, observed that "*fucking* was used adjectivally to qualify almost every noun in the soldier's vocabulary." (More evidence that swearing is probably linked with male violence, drinking, domination, and warmongering.)

Allen Walker Read wrote one of the earliest and most thorough monographs on the f-word—"An Obscenity Symbol," published in *American Speech* in 1934—fifteen pages and eighty-two footnotes about the dirty word, without once printing it anywhere in the article. Instead, Read refers throughout to "our word," "this word," "the most disreputable of all English words," and so on. Read had this to say about the military man's indiscriminate use of the most obscene word:

> The soldier, compelled to outrage his inmost nature by killing his fellow human beings, found

life topsy-turvy in so many respects that it is small wonder that his observance of taboo was in the inverted manner. The supporters of a civilization that can send forth its young men to kill each other ought not to be squeamish about the misuse of a few words. With nerves relentlessly exacerbated by gunfire, the unnatural way of life, and the imminence of a hideous death, the soldier could find fitting expression only in terms that according to teaching from his childhood were foul and disgusting.

Swearing has been with us since the first caveperson bumped her or his head on her or his way out to take a piss —probably before words, wars, words of war, and wars of words were invented. As Steven Pinker noted recently in *The Language Instinct,* language production takes place in the so-called higher structures of the human brain, the cerebral cortex, primarily the left perisylvian region. Swearing, by contrast, is controlled not in the cerebral cortex, but by the so-called lower, subcortical structures in the brain stem and limbic system, structures "older" in evolutionary time and more primitive, associated with aggression and emotions—the same neural structures that control the vocal calls of primates. Swearing is a different kind of language, controlled by a different part of the brain. Lesions in the "higher" speech centers of the cerebral cortex often cause aphasia (loss or impairment of the ability to use words as symbols), but as Pinker notes, "many aphasics are superb at swearing."

Researchers at the University of Pennsylvania recently compared the brains of men and women using Positron Emission Tomography scans. The studies confirm what everybody already knew: that men use these lower, more primitive limbic regions of the brain more than women do. Thus, we may conclude that male brains are wired for violence and swearing.

So men are actually innocent victims of biology and neural Darwinism. Swearing erupts from our intact, primate unconscious; it's our lower selves making preverbal sounds that originate in the same parts of the brain responsible for weeping, laughing, groaning, and crying out in pain.

William Gass, a novelist and essayist, explored blue language in a diamond of a book, *On Being Blue,* full of unusual insights about swearing and why we do it, including a fascinating gender-specific analysis of the exhortation "Fuck you." He recalls saying "Fuck you" to the backside of a traffic cop and proceeds to explicate his own utterance:

> **Fuck-yous are in fact the principal item of macho exchange. Since I do not want to fuck the cop I must want someone else to, and since that ubiquitous "you" is almost certainly another male (as it is in this instance), I can only desire your sodomization. To be entered as a woman**

is to be so demeaned and reduced and degraded:
for us gaucho machos, what could be worse? In
a business deal, if you have been screwed, what
should have been *up theirs* is disconcertingly *up
you.*

The commercial connotations of "fucking" someone—
as in cheating, victimizing, deceiving, or betraying them—
go way back, but probably the first written appearance of
this sense of the word comes from a deposition taken over
a hundred years ago, in 1866: "Mr. Baker replied that the
deponent would be *fucked* out of his money by Mr. Brown."
Carefully preserving this historic moment, the notary public made an entry following the use of the word *fucked* in
the transcript:

> Before putting down the word as used by the
> witness, I requested him to reflect upon the lan-
> guage he attributed to Mr. Baker, and not to
> impute to him an outrage upon all that was
> decent. The witness reitterated [*sic*] it, and said
> that it was the word used by Mr. Baker. [*Ran-
> dom House Historical Dictionary of American
> Slang*]

Almost all dirty-word antiquarians agree with Gass that
"Fuck you!" has very little to do with cupidity or heterosexual copulation, and indeed probably has much more to do
with the abject humiliation of enforced buggery. "Fuck you"

is a male curse, thrown like a brickbat at a deserving ass-hole. Thus, an evil turn of events or a sudden run of misfortune may be commemorated by the expression "Ain't that a fuck in the ass!" And as one maledictive specialist has noted, fuck's anal-aggressive overtones have a very long history:

> *Fuck you!* ... replaces the older reference to hell & damnation in an age of unfaith. It is probably short for *I fuck you,* or *I fuck you in the ass,* a threat or insult that goes back to Ancient Egypt, where the god Min actually carries out this threat on one of his enemies, who then has a baby (Thoth) born from his forehead. The myths of Dionysus being born from Jupiter's thigh—and Eve from Adam's rib—are simply later and more polite versions of this. [G. Gershon Legman, "A Word for It," in *The Best of Maledicta*]

Legman also tells us that, instead of a notary public's seal, "Egyptian legal documents of the last dynasties used to be reinforced ... with the stereotyped phrase: 'As for him who shall disregard it, *may he be fucked by a donkey.*' The hieroglyphic for this curse makes the matter unmistakably clear with two little drawings of large, erect penises."

So men swear and say "Fuck you!" because they are violent and competitive, and women swear less often because they are benevolent and vindictive. Certain women avoid on-the-spot confrontations, slink away, nourish their grudges, and accumulate evidence, waiting for the opportunity to file a lawsuit, smear a candidate for high office, or accuse a nominee for the Supreme Court. Is this better or worse than a prompt and thorough cussing out?

Before Camille Paglia formulated her Top 40 persona, there was another intelligent, trenchant observer of the politics of victim feminism in the person of Florence King, author of *With Charity Toward None: Confessions of a Misanthrope:*

> The best way to bottle up anger is to turn men into women. After years of consensus seeking, reaching out, coming together, building bridges, linking arms, and tying yellow ribbons, the feminization of America is now complete. American men have been turned into their own secret police, under orders to kick down their own doors in the middle of the night and arrest themselves for "insensitivity." . . .
>
> The feminization of America is so pervasive that it has even changed the way men talk, not just their tones but the whole thrust of their conversations. Persuaded that normal masculine directness and unequivocality might make people *angry,* today's men have adopted the age-old feminine stratagem of hurt feelings and the newer feminist technique of politicized nagging to get their point across. Our national discourse now is conducted in a baritone tsk-tsking tut-

tuttery, as when a snippy Dan Rather demanded of his man in Alaska: "Did Hazelwood ever apologize for the Valdez oil spill?"

Men swear. Women nag. Rush Limbaugh and Howard Stern hurl epithets and ad hominem rotten tomatoes. Catherine MacKinnon and Andrea Dworkin issue incessant remonstrations, tirelessly and selflessly defending the rights of the group to which they belong. As Florence King observed, radical feminism gives a closet misanthrope an excuse for despising half of the human race, and most radical feminists give men the distinct impression that they would merrily tiptoe through fifty male corpses to interview one woman whose low self-esteem is Barbie-induced and whose husband threatened to punch her on Super Bowl Sunday.

Why is a woman obsessed with women's issues any more exalted than a man obsessed with male ones? A female candidate running on a platform consisting of women's issues, such as abortion rights and antipornography legislation, is a civil rights hero. If a male candidate were stupid enough to run on a platform consisting only of men's issues, such as equal custody and visitation in divorce decrees and the father's right to veto a mother's abortion decisions, he would be called a male chauvinist pig.

Swearing is becoming illegal in the workplace precisely because men do it more than women. And women find it offensive, in the same way men can't stand nagging. When the Supreme Court and the EEOC make federal rules forbidding "ridicule" and "verbal insult" in the workplace (something men have endured for centuries with no re-dress), the law is designed to have the same equitable result that Anatole France put his finger on when he observed that "the law, in its majestic equality, forbids the rich as well as the poor to sleep under bridges, to beg in the streets, and to steal bread."

Let's go back to that sensitivity training session at work. Unless you want to swallow hard, smile at the gender-equity specialist, and think of something sensitive to say, the only possible recourse is to exercise your remaining civil rights and say:

"Ma'am, the first two amendments to the United States Constitution give me the federally guaranteed right to swear and keep loaded guns in my house. Now, unless you've gone and called a constitutional convention and I missed reading about it in the paper, please don't tell me that the govern-ment says I can't say certain words, and that I must say certain others instead.

"I hope I haven't offended any of the girls or ladies. And I will try not to swear, ridicule, insult, or say anything offensive. In fact, I will make you a deal. I won't swear, ridicule, insult, or say anything offensive, unless you tell me I can't because it's illegal, in which case I am going to go home and write an entire book containing nothing but the most ridiculous, insulting, and offensive things I can think of. Then I am going to read it out loud every time you tell me it's against the law."

Look It Up

*Leaf through a dictionary or try to make one, and you
will find that every word covers and masks a well so
bottomless that the questions you toss into it arouse no
more than an echo.*

—PAUL VALÉRY, ANALECTS

*W*ebster's *New World Dictionary,* Second College Edition,
was published in 1970 and did not include definitions for
dago, kike, wop, wog, and various other slurs. Dr. David B.
Guralnik, editor in chief at the time, justified the exclusion
of these words in an editorial statement:

> It was decided in the selection process that this
> dictionary could easily dispense with those true
> obscenities, the terms of racial or ethnic oppro-
> brium, that are, in any case, encountered with
> diminishing frequency these days.

What halcyon times we live in, when people such as Dr. Guralnik think they can help to remedy ancient hatreds with a little word surgery, a *logos*-ectomy to remove offensive words and the hateful thoughts lurking behind them. Maybe we should remove the religious slurs and racial epithets from all the dictionaries in Bosnia and see if the civil war ends.

For centuries, *fuck* was the most objectionable word in the English language, but now *nigger* and *cunt* are probably tied for that distinction, and *fuck* has at long last stepped down. Finally, hatred is more dangerous than sex. As the deputy district attorney in the O. J. Simpson case, Christopher Darden, recently told us and Judge Lance Ito, the word *nigger* "is the dirtiest, filthiest, nastiest word in the English language, and it has no place in a courtroom."

Fuck was kept out of print and out of dictionaries for hundreds of years for being the dirtiest, filthiest, nastiest word in the English language. Is it time to take *nigger* and *cunt* out of our dictionaries? Because they are just too offensive, abusive, objectionable? It's not a silly question.

If Mark Twain's and Flannery O'Connor's books haven't been burned by the year 2050, what will happen when twenty-first-century readers look up *nigger* in their dictionaries? Will they be able to find a record of the word's meanings? How innocuous it seemed at the end of the nineteenth century? How malicious, hateful, and utterly offensive it was in the latter part of the twentieth? How it was used in the African-American community as a term of affection and endearment?

This kind of historical inquiry requires distance. We are too close to *nigger* and *cunt.* They are still so charged that a tour of their etymologies and usages would be too painful for us, even in a book as self-consciously confrontational as this one. To gain a real appreciation for the deleterious effects of word discrimination and bans on "verbal conduct," we need a word like *fuck,* whose alarming vigor is still in recent memory, but whose recent ascent in the modern vernacular makes it less odious than others. I don't mean to discriminate against similarly situated swearwords. As we'll see in later chapters, other formerly objectionable maledictions, such as *shit* or *hell,* are extremely important and are now so approachable they can be downright fascinating. I confine myself for the moment to the f-word because it's still a "dirty" word, and we can study its persecution at the hands of numskulls and prudes in other centuries without making ourselves sick on rage, fear, and indignation.

The f-word is also convenient for our purposes, because the exciting new slang dictionaries are multivolume compendiums—so vast in their scope that only their early volumes are currently available. (There are just too many interesting dirty words to cover in a single volume.) At this writing, the *Random House Historical Dictionary of American Slang* (J. E. Lighter, editor) contains only one volume, A–G, and the *Dictionary of American Regional English* (Frederic G. Cassidy and Joan Hall: Harvard/Belknap Press) consists of two volumes, A–C and D–H. *Fuck* falls within the ambits of both, whereas *shit* will have to wait for coverage in later volumes, which may not be out for years. (Don't worry, in a little while you can put on hip waders, and we'll go off foraging in the verdant pastures of *shit,* where the likes of Mr. Lighter and Mr. Cassidy and Ms. Hall have yet to tread.)

The f-word still does not appear in most dictionaries, or it merits an entry or two, though it rivals almost any other word in the language for sheer versatility and frequency of use—at least when men are doing the talking. We can print the word in full here and discuss it at some length, because this is a men's book, and men swear a lot. (Readers please note, this is not a sexist comment. As we will see, a sexist comment is one that implies women are inferior to men. A comment implying that men are inferior pigs who express surprise or astonishment by exclaiming, *"Holy fuck!"* is simply an accurate observation.)

No matter what the dictionary, rivers of print are wasted at each and every entry telling the reader that *fuck* is "usu. considered vulgar," or "usu. considered obscene," just in case the reader is a member of the Ukit tribe just off the plane from Borneo. I'm not being paid by the word, so I'll begin with a blanket, cigarette-pack warning:

ANY PHRASE OR EXPRESSION CONTAINING THE WORD
FUCK IS USUALLY CONSIDERED VULGAR AND OBSCENE!

Dictionaries ignored the f-word for centuries, because it was absolutely taboo, and often even illegal. For almost four hundred years, scholars smitten with a catholic love for words, who otherwise jealously guarded their academic freedoms, who religiously followed the spirit of inquiry wherever it led them, were easily cowed by prudery and popular tastes into omitting *fuck* from their dictionaries.

Dr. Samuel Johnson—father of the English language and maker of its first dictionary—once said a lexicographer is "a harmless drudge that busies himself in tracing the original, and detailing the signification of words." Not all words, it would seem, because we do not find the dirty ones in Johnson's famous *Dictionary of the English Language* (1755). Maybe Johnson meant to say a maker of dictionaries is a drudge defining harmless words, for he quietly omitted most of the offensive words of his day, and was squeamish about including even the mildly unpleasant ones. In his preface, written in 1755, Johnson observed: "As politeness increases, some expressions will be considered as too gross and vulgar for the delicate."

Although Johnson was theoretically chaste, a popular anecdote suggests he was aware of certain colorful expressions not found in his own dictionary. He told a story about his mother and how she had once called him a puppy. Johnson was only a boy at the time, but he had responded by asking her if she knew what they called a puppy's mother.

After Johnson's dictionary was published, a literary lady complimented him upon it and expressed her satisfaction that he had not admitted any improper words (as Hugh Rawson points out in *Wicked Words: A Treasury of Curses, Insults, Put-Downs, and Other Formerly Unprintable Terms from Anglo-Saxon Times to the Present*—*bloody, bum,* and *fart* seemed not to have ruffled her feathers). "No, Madam," Johnson replied, "I hope I have not daubed my fingers. I find, however, that you have been looking for them."

It is as if eighteenth-century society matrons had convinced Linnaeus—the founder of the binomial system of scientific classification of plants and animals—not to classify snails and to simply omit any mention of them in biology texts. Because snails are unsightly creatures, sticky and repulsive, their presence would defile every other one of God's creatures, and therefore snails shall not be assigned to any known genera or species.

Or as Allen Walker Read observed:

> A sociologist does not refuse to study certain criminals on the ground that they are too perverted or too dastardly; surely a student of language is even less warranted in refusing to consider certain four-letter words because they are too "nasty" or too "dirty."

To this we might add that the Centers for Disease Control do not forbid the study of certain diseases because their etiology is somehow unspeakable, or because they deal with parts of the body better left unexplored, lest physicians sully themselves with body parts used for nasty activities. In the name of "healing," medical science has somehow put itself above questions of vulgarity or indiscretion. One wonders why the same empirical license has never been endowed on word scientists, when, as St. John tells us, "the word" (divine and also all too human) has been with us from the beginning, and is more important to our humanity than urinary tract infections and venereal diseases.

Yet, one after another, philologists and lexicographers succumbed to the popular superstitions and excluded the dirtiest word from their lexicons. Even the redoubtable H. L. Mencken, a guy you could count on to raise hell during High Mass, skips from *fubar* to *fudge* in the index to *The American Language,* published in 1934, and dances around the f-word while discussing *fubar* ("fouled" or "foozled up beyond all recognition") by referring to it as the word "beginning with f." Still more incredible, Mencken wrote an article for the journal *American Speech* in 1944 entitled "American Profanity," without printing the word, or even alluding to it, as far as I could tell. True, it was illegal for publishers to print the word at the time, but other word scholars found ways to refer to it, or used the expedient of asterisks and dashes, which *The New York Times* uses to this day.

A dirty-word hero whose work we explore later in this precious volume, Dr. Leo Stone, a psychiatrist and author of "On the Principal Obscene Word of the English Language" (*International Journal of Psycho-Analysis* XXXV, 1954, pp. 30–54), stated flatly and authoritatively that, in 1954, "no reliable American or English general dictionaries now current contain the word." At that time, Stone complained that he had also consulted a "considerable number of dictionaries devoted to vulgar language without finding it."

It wasn't until five years later, in 1959, just after baby

boomers had attained the age of reason, that Grove Press, a publisher, sued and won the right to print the f-word in D. H. Lawrence's *Lady Chatterley's Lover*.

The casual vulgarian may shrug his shoulders at the systematic, invidious discrimination that kept the f-word out of dictionaries for five hundred years. Only word historians and linguists appreciate the damage done by centuries of neglect: specifically, we have no history of the word's meanings; we cannot study its evolution, where it came from, why it has stayed so long, why it has outlasted other coarse, monosyllabic synonyms, such as *jape* or *sard*, and just when in etymological time it acquired its pungent taboo. Think of the centuries that have gone by, with not a single lexicographer willing to provide *fuck* with a printed cage in the word menageries known as dictionaries. The record of the word's youth is lost forever!

As Justice Oliver Wendell Holmes observed: "A word is not a crystal, transparent and unchanged; it is the skin of a living thought and may vary greatly in color and content according to the circumstances and the time in which it is used." Holmes was arguing the changeableness of the word *income,* which meant something different when used in a turn-of-the-century revenue act than it meant when used in the Sixteenth Amendment.

Imagine the unrecorded thoughts that have lived and breathed for centuries under the skin of our orphaned word! If Valéry is right, and every word in a dictionary is simply the cover of a bottomless well, what happens when the word is not there? For hundreds of years? Thanks to centuries of censorship, we lack even an echo when we go spelunking in the barren archives of the second-dirtiest word.

Or think of words as bottles of wine, as Hugh Rawson did: "The wine may change as it ages, and people may argue about whether it is really good or bad." But we do not therefore make it illegal to pronounce the names of certain wines.

Like Johnson's admirer, I have sullied my fingers looking for dirty words in dictionaries. My *Webster's Third New International Dictionary, Unabridged*—the fat tome one often sees open on lecterns in libraries—coyly skips from *fuchsite* (noun—a mineral consisting of a common mica containing chromium) to *fucoid* (adjective—of, relating to, or resembling algae of the order Fucales). At least Merriam-Webster was consistent: they would neither define *fuck* nor use it to define another word, as evidenced by their definition of *snafu,* a slang military acronym originating in England during World War II, meaning "Situation Normal All Fucked Up." Merriam-Webster opted for the drawing-room version, using "Fouled Up" and avoiding the f-word.

A separately published 1983 supplement to the same volume, entitled *9,000 Words,* lists *fuck* as a verb, as well as a noun ("used esp. with *the* as a meaningless intensive"). It also features *fucked-up, fucker, fuck off, fuck over, fuck up* as a verb, and *fuckup* as a noun. A 1993 edition of the same dictionary lists these same plain-label examples in the addenda, without a single addition. Sprinkled throughout the bare-boned definitions are the usual officious warnings:

WARNING! USU. CONSIDERED OBSCENE! DO NOT TRY USING *FUCK* AT HOME! THE EDITORS OF THIS DICTIONARY ARE SLANG PROFESSIONALS. DO NOT REMOVE THIS TAG! RISK OF SHOCK! DO NOT OPEN OR ATTEMPT TO SERVICE THIS WORD UNIT UNLESS YOU ARE A QUALIFIED LINGUISTIC TECHNICIAN! THIS IS A DICTIONARY, NOT A LADDER, AND *FUCK* IS NOT A STEP! IF USE OF THIS WORD PERSISTS FOR MORE THAN 48 HOURS CONSULT YOUR PHYSICIAN!

Compared to the plethora of *fuck* definitions found in even the most basic slang dictionary, this mere handful can only be called a tentative foray on the part of the Merriam-Webster editorial staff, a blushing admission that at least one dirty word exists, and that it can be used in several different senses. Ten years have passed since Webster's decided to admit that *fuck* exists, but in their 1993 addenda they still studiously deny the reader a single example of usage.

Webster's must be staffed by humorless word technicians who are resolutely literal and willfully tone deaf to any suggestion of vulgarity. If you could somehow intrude at the appropriate moment on their wedding night and ask them to please define "pulsating organ" and "interrupted screw," they would roll over, raise up on their elbows, and matter-of-factly advise that the former is "a minute muscular organ functioning as an accessory heart in various insects," and the latter is "a screw with longitudinal cuts through the threads." Don't ask if their throbbing nether parts and what you just did to them bring anything else to mind.

The neglect inflicted on dirty words by every renowned dictionary from *The Oxford English Dictionary* (which nowadays features a respectable selection) to *Roget's International Thesaurus* (which left the f-word out of the fourth edition but included it in the recently released fifth) is a long, sad tale. What is the First Amendment if not an attempt to confer civil rights on words, which provide the currency of exchange in the bond markets of human interaction?

Instead of belaboring *fuck*'s status as a victim and concocting a whining screed on behalf of its "equality rights" as a word that has been discriminated against for centuries, I will instead proclaim the glass of etymology half full and celebrate the new slang dictionaries—massive, multivolume scholarly undertakings—which provide the occasion for a fresh look at the f-word and, for the first time in the history of Western Civilization, a chance to learn about profanity from real word experts.

Swearing is not for polite conversation, and that's the fun of it. It can be extremely entertaining, if it's done well. But where does one learn how to do it better? Answer: rowdy bars and the new slang dictionaries, both of which acquaint the novice practitioner with the essentials of vocabulary, usage, and phraseology.

But keep in mind the lesson learned by Mark Twain's wife when she attempted to cure him of his renowned habit of cursing. She made notes on the vast repertoire of his prolific profanity, then studied and memorized as many expressions as she could. At the next opportunity, under the pretext of being put out by some trifling annoyance, she gave Twain a dose of his own medicine by repeating his own curses back to him, as many as she could recall.

Twain's reply: "Olivia, my dear, you know all the words but you haven't got the tune."

Words alone won't cut it. Setting, timing, and technique are also extremely important. It takes a literary genius like James Joyce to elevate common name-calling to an art form: "I'll wring the bastard fucker's bleeding blasted fucking windpipe!" (*Ulysses*). The rest of us sometimes have to make do with sheer density of vulgarity, which can be exhilarating: "The fuckin fucker's fucked, fer fuck sakes!" (Andreas Schroeder, *Shaking It Rough*, 1976), which makes you want to find this Schroeder fellow and pour him a few drinks, so you can meet the singular intelligence capable of fitting four fucks into a seven-word sentence.

One should be careful to select an ambience with lots of decorum and plenty of politeness and good manners. This will nicely accentuate your own vulgar speech, your bad attitude, and your profound insensitivity to others—in short, it will make your swearing really count for something. And, of course, one must assiduously cultivate the previously mentioned habits of rowdy bars and slang dictionaries.

With regard to the former, one could do worse than follow the example of the erudite antiquarian Francis Grose, author of *A Classical Dictionary of the Vulgar Tongue*, published in 1785, the first and boldest dictionary of English slang.

Grose was a rotund gourmand, an "antiquarian Falstaff" according to one source, a man who could "eat with Sancho, and drink with the Knight" according to another, a master of "banter and jovial ridicule," who could "set the table on a roar." He was a creature of diverse and scrimmaging appetites, one of which was an insatiable craving for vulgarity. Driven by the collector's mania, Grose sallied forth each midnight into the slums of St. Giles in search of adventures and the vulgar speech of adventurers.

According to Eric Partridge—probably the foremost collector of slang in the history of the English language—who wrote a biographical sketch appended to a new edition of *Vulgar Tongue,* Grose "was extremely fond of taking his porter of an evening at the King's Arms . . . a house distinguished for the company of wits, men of talent, and the most respectable tradesmen in the neighborhood."

From the King's Arms, Partridge tells us, Grose and his companions frequently started at midnight and went into the Back Slums, where they made themselves as "affable and jolly as the rest of the motley crew among the beggars, cadgers, thieves, etc., who at that time infested the 'Holy Land' [St. Giles district]." From there they went to the "Scout-Kens" [the so-called watch houses], "on the 'lookout' for a bit of fun . . . and the dirty 'smoke pipes' in Turnmill Street . . . in his search after character. Neither were the rough squad at St. Kitts, and the sailor-boys capering ashore at Saltpetre Bank, forgotten in their nightly strolls."

> In short, wherever a "bit of life" could be seen
> to advantage, or the "knowledge-box" . . . ob-
> tain anything like a new light respecting man-
> kind, he felt himself happy, and did not think
> his time misapplied. It was from these nocturnal
> sallies, and the slang expressions which continu-
> ally assailed his ears, that Francis Grose was first
> induced to compile *A Classical Dictionary of the
> Vulgar Tongue.*

There you have it. The perfect excuse next time you head
out at midnight and she wakes up just in time to stop you
at the door.

"Where are you going?"

"Uh, I'm going to meet some guys for a beer at the
King's Arms, I mean, the Queen's Legs. Forget it, I'm on my
way to a support group at the Monarch's Limbs."

"It's after midnight!"

"Honey, I'm sallying forth in search of colorful characters, to see a bit of life to advantage, to replenish my knowledge box, to seek a new light respecting people-kind, and,
above all, to record slang expressions that assail my ears in
the bars and pool halls, so I can make a new edition of the
Classical Dictionary of the Vulgar Tongue. Believe me, I'd
rather stay here and get a good night's sleep. This is work!
I'm only doing it for you and the kids. Random House is
paying me for this!"

Francis Grose recorded one of the first official definitions of the f-word, listing it as "TO F--K. To copulate."

Grose's *Vulgar Tongue* displays the usual incongruity between what is allowed and what is deemed to be too offensive at any given time in the history of the English language, for in the same volume one finds *burning shame* defined as "a lighted candle stuck into the parts of a woman, certainly not intended by nature for a candlestick," and *beard splitter* as "A man much given to wenching." To modern sensibilities these are at least ten times as offensive as seeing all four letters of the f-word strung together. And if Grose showed up at work tomorrow morning and started defining eighteenth-century English slang for the edification of the human resources department at XYZ Corporation, his lawyer's advice would be to stop dreaming about getting off and start planning for liability—individual liability for triple punitive damages, a stretch in a minimum-security facility, followed by years of community service and biweekly sensitivity workshops run by Oprah, Phil, and Kathie Lee.

The modern slang dictionaries celebrate words in a fashion Grose—if he could somehow come back to life—would find infinitely amusing, and which he might even conclude more than make up for the centuries of invidious discrimination inflicted on his treasury of vulgar expressions. Even in Grose's day, most dictionaries could easily avoid saying anything about the f-word in the interest of propriety, but no such luxury is available to the editors of slang dictionaries. They must make a decision about the extent of their coverage. The safest and most common course is to offer a restrained, dignified catalogue featuring only the most common and unimaginative uses of *fuck,* such as *fucked up, fucked over, fucking*—as a verbal noun, an adjective, an adverb—*what the fuck?, fuck off,* and so on, each illustrated with one colorless example of usage, and then move on to *fud.*

Because this approach is so common, the slang lover is completely unprepared for the *Random House Historical Dictionary of American Slang.* It offers a veritable fuckfest of variations, applications, and creative employments for the use of the dirtiest word, and a fuck of a lot more. Each definition is accompanied by a multitude of usage examples covering nearly five hundred years of artful swearing. Pages 830 to 842 of dense, double-columned type cover *fuck* and its derivatives, including *fuckish, fuckable, fuckaholic, fuck-stick, fuck-struck, fuckbag, fuck-nutty,* and to *fuck up a wet dream,* meaning to be exceedingly clumsy or stupid.

If you are doing field research on *fuck* as a transitive verb, your partner might want to know that there is no evidence to support the assumption of many educated people that *fuck* is an Anglo-Saxon word. On the contrary, it is probably an English reflex of a widespread Germanic form, related also to Middle Dutch *fokken,* "to thrust, copulate with," Norwegian *fukka,* and Swiss *focka,* "to strike, push, copulate," but the lack of old citations makes the etymology impossible to trace, thanks to the thorough efforts of word gestapos in other centuries.

Random House also has a well-developed social conscience. In the course of defining *go fuck (yourself)* (frequently varied by substituting other objects), the editors admonish us that *"Go fuck your mother* is universally perceived as the most offensive and provocative idiomatic imprecation in English." My advice is to avoid it entirely because it sounds positively cliché compared to the other featured examples: *Go and fuck rattlesnakes. Go fuck thy suffering self.* "Fuck yourself. Fuck your mother. Fuck your sister" (Hemingway, "Winner Take Nothing," 1932). "God fuck old Bennet" (Joyce, *Ulysses*). And if none of those work, try: "Aw, go fuck your mother in bed, you little prick" (attributed to a thirteen-year-old New York City schoolboy circa 1959). (F-word aficionados unable to afford the fifty-dollar cover price of the Random House slang dictionary may purchase all of its *fuck*-related entries in an amusing, erudite little volume called—what else?—*The F Word,* edited by Jesse Sheidlower.)

The *Dictionary of American Regional English,* now in its second volume, D–H, contains a mere four entries for *fuck* and its related words and phrases. The selection ignores all of the more common embodiments and instead focuses on a handful of idiosyncratic uses, lively and curious to be sure, but strangely isolated. (Slang enthusiasts please note that *DARE* makes up for its slim *fuck* pickings with almost six twin-columned pages of entries on *hell* and derivative phrases.)

The first *DARE* contribution is *fuck bug,* a noun hailing from rural Louisiana, where it is used to refer to "little orange and black bugs that come out in great numbers, always coupled, during the summer." This is followed by *fuck bump,* "an inflamed pimple," and we are urged to look at *love bump* and *nature bump* for comparison.

The highly entertaining verb phrase *fuck the dog* (*fucking the dog,* verbal noun), meaning "to loaf, shirk work; to malinger," is covered in full. A catalogue of examples includes uses from all parts of the country, ranging in meaning from "doing little unimportant things," to malingering, goldbricking, to "wasting time and loafing on the job."

From Weaver, Texas, comes the example "Mike is the world champion at fuckin' the dog. I found him yesterday asleep under a truck with his sunglasses on and his hands wired to the driveshaft so it'd look like he was workin'."

Last in line from *DARE* is *fucky-knuckle,* an adverbial phrase describing the manner in which one shoots a marble in marble play: "Shooting with the taw cradled against the index finger so that the taw was pushed out with the thumb was called shooting fucky-knuckle." We'll have to wait for later volumes to tell us what *taw* means, because we are boycotting Merriam-Webster, which probably defines *taw,* but won't tell us about *fucky-knuckle.*

Adding European flair to your swearing can startle the most jaded listener, and the British are no slugs when it comes to profanity. Eric Partridge, a true slang pioneer, created the first *Dictionary of Slang and Unconventional English* back in 1936, and it is presently in its eighth edition. We learn that Shakespeare contains nine transitive synonyms for the f-word, five intransitive.

In England, to *create fuck* means "to make a considerable fuss, usually in protest." To *fuck about* is to "play the fool."

A *fuck-beggar* is "an impotent or almost impotent man whom none but a beggar-woman will allow to kiss her."

A theatrical invention—*fuck her while she's (still) hot*—is "reputedly the gallery's response in blood and thunder melodramas, when the hero, wringing his hands at the fate of the (apparently) dead heroine, implored, 'What shall I do?' "

Fuck-in-a-fog is a "low, jocular" name for the flower otherwise known as love-in-a-mist. To the routine exclamation of "Fuck me!" the British supply handy, catchphrase responses in the form of "Not now," or "Later," or "No thanks." Variations include *Fuck me and the baby's yours! Fuck me gently! Fuck me pink! Fuck me said the Duchess more in hope than in expectation.* The latter forms the "start of a coarse monologue, the next line being usually, '*What, not again,' said the Duke wearily.*"

Fuck my luck! means "Oh! What a pity!" *Fuck my old boots!* proclaims the usual astonishment; a humorous euphemism for the same is "Seduce my ancient footwear."

A *fuck-pig* is a thoroughly unpleasant person (usually a man). To be *fucked in the car* or *fucked without getting kissed* both "connote that someone has done something to you that you did not deserve." A sexually desirable woman may be described as *fucksome*. A *fuckster* or *fuckstress* is "a notable performer of, an addict to, the sexual act."

My attorneys have advised me to conclude with another warning for the hapless reader who may have breezed by the first warning in his earnest to get to the examples of usage:

ANY PHRASE OR EXPRESSION CONTAINING THE WORD *FUCK* IS USUALLY CONSIDERED VULGAR AND OBSCENE. THIS BOOK CONTAINS VULGAR, OBSCENE, ABUSIVE, AND OFFENSIVE WORDS—LOTS OF THEM—SOME-TIMES DOZENS ON A SINGLE PAGE. IF YOU READ THIS BOOK AND ARE OFFENDED OR EMOTIONALLY DIS-TRESSED YOU WILL NOT BE ENTITLED TO ANY JUDG-MENT IN A COURT OF LAW.

IF YOU READ THIS BOOK AND USE ANY DIRTY OR OFFENSIVE WORDS BECAUSE THE AUTHOR INTENTION-ALLY SUGGESTED IT WAS APPROPRIATE, OR BECAUSE YOU FIND THE WORDS TO BE ATTRACTIVE NUISANCES, OR BECAUSE THE AUTHOR COERCED YOU INTO USING FILTHY LANGUAGE BY MENTALLY ABUSING YOU, YOU WILL STILL BE SUED FOR SEXUAL HARASSMENT AND INTENTIONAL INFLICTION OF EMOTIONAL DISTRESS AND YOU WILL LOSE. YOU WILL BE PROSECUTED FOR HATE-SPEECH CRIMES, THEN YOU WILL SUFFER HOR-RIBLY, AND DIE A SLOW, AGONIZING DEATH—ALL PROXIMATELY CAUSED BY THE MENTAL DISTRESS OF READING THIS BOOK, AND STILL YOU WILL HAVE NO LEGAL COURSE OF ACTION AGAINST THE AUTHOR OR PUBLISHER OF THIS BOOK.

PROCEED AT YOUR OWN RISK, AND ONLY IF YOU FIRST AGREE THAT ANY CASE YOU BRING AGAINST THE

AUTHOR OR PUBLISHER OF THIS BOOK WILL BE
THROWN OUT OF COURT, BECAUSE YOU AGREE IN AD-
VANCE THAT BY PROCEEDING YOU ARE CRIMINALLY
AND CONTRIBUTORILY NEGLIGENT.

But, as we have discussed, let the newest rash of Peck-sniffery and speech regulations be an incentive for the liberal use of vulgarities. Holding forth with a few contemptibly loud *fuck*s every now and again reminds people that, for the time being, we may indulge in free speech whenever we like. We are not yet put outside with the cigarette smokers during our fifteen-minute breaks. But the day is fast approaching when all speech will be regulated in the interest of civil rights and the prosecution of hate criminals, who commit gender crimes through the hostile and abusive use of illegal words.

The *fuck* you don't say today will be one you won't be allowed to say tomorrow.

Dirty-Word Psycholinguistics

Dirty words as well as dreams are a true way to the unconscious. They provide, like the old roads built by the government, wider and more perfect access to the hidden world.

—SANDOR FERENCZI, "ON OBSCENE WORDS," IN *SEX IN PSYCHO-ANALYSIS*

*T*his observation, from one of Freud's most notable pupils, shows how attempts to censor swearing or the use of offensive words are nothing short of assaults on the human psyche. Imagine a statute forbidding the discussion of nightmares, or legislation banning laughter inspired by the misfortunes of others, and the implications of harassment laws forbidding the use of ridicule, insults, and hostility become clear. As we'll see later, even unremarkable, coarse epithets such as *shit* or *hell* are fraught with fundamental human fears and truths. Once the word police succeed in making it illegal to call someone a bitch, a nigger, a bastard, an old fart, a queer, a wetback, a klutz, a fatty, a cripple, or a kike, the next logical baby step is to make it illegal to call someone a worthless piece of shit. And then what?

Even Freud knew that dirty words and "anal-emissive speech" are more than substitutes for sexual aggression. Vulgar speech may be verbal fallout from primal scenes and polymorphously perverse childhood traumas, but swearing is also the close cousin of magic, ritual, laughter, dreams, neurosis, and reflex—all indispensable expressions of instincts and impulses. Repressed instincts usually signal their presence by slips of the tongue, by jokes, and by dirty words. Disordered personalities express themselves with disordered speech. But detecting and then banning disordered speech does not heal the neurotic any more than criminals can be identified by handwriting analysis or reformed by penmanship lessons. If anything, closing off the mind's ventilation systems may bestir the seeds of madness to germinate and blossom in the raging hothouse of insanity.

Since Freud's time, personality disorders have become even more important to modern mental health, because without them social scientists would be unable to supplement their academic stipends with government-reimbursed counseling fees, and the entire profession would vanish. (One thinks of Karl Kraus's remark that "the relation between psychiatrists and other kinds of lunatics is more or less the relation of a convex folly to a concave one.")

There's a long-standing philosophical argument about whether we use speech to convey thoughts or to hide them. Either way, the inveterate potty mouth is suspect. Dirty words present a classical linguistic problem: What do they *mean*? Or is that the wrong question? The great philosopher Ludwig Wittgenstein came very close to terminal despair in his love affair with words and his obsession with thorny, linguistic dilemmas when he was forced to conclude that it is almost impossible to *say* anything. His recommended approach to resolving the mystery of any given word: "Don't ask for the meaning, ask for the use."

This puts him in the company of many a steadfast vulgarian, for dirty-word users don't much care about the technical meaning of the words they use, any more than a delinquent cares what kind of rock he is throwing through the windshield of his neighbor's car, or what color of paper he chews to make the spitballs he hurls. As William Gass observed, "All these anal-sex-and-smear swears serve the same function, and are largely interchangeable like turds, for one stool is as good as another in the democracy of the mouth." Instead of wallowing in self-esteem and admiring the diversity of the human race, the user of dirty words projects his misanthropy on the world in the form of filthy words, and practitioners bill him for the therapy required to identify and uncover the sources of his hatefulness.

With all this unconscious activity clustering around the fear and deployment of dirty words, it should come as no surprise that psychoanalysts, psychiatrists, and psycholinguists were pioneers in exploring vulgarity, and some of these learned people even managed to get a few opinions about dirty words into print. Even before the Supreme

Court's landmark obscenity decisions, two notable dirty-word experts were especially brave and thorough in bringing the f-word into its modern fashion and earning its rightful place in our nation's dictionaries. The aforementioned Allen Walker Read, in "An Obscenity Symbol," included everything you would want to know about the f-word, except how to spell it. Although he stopped short of printing it, Read made more than a few sage, psycholinguistic observations, including the notion that obscenity is found not so much in words or things, but in the *attitudes* people have toward supposedly obscene words or things:

> To hazard a definition, we may say that obscenity is any reference to the bodily functions that gives to anyone a certain emotional reaction, that of a "fearful thrill" in seeing, doing, or speaking the forbidden. Thus it is the existence of a ban or taboo that creates the obscenity where none existed before.

What Read called a "fearful thrill," Freud called a "sacred fear" in *Totem and Taboo,* where we learn that *taboo* comes to us from Polynesia, and that it has two precisely opposite meanings, both of which are reflected in the first two definitions found in *Webster's Third:* (1) "set apart as venerable or as charged with a dangerous supernatural power: forbidden to profane use or contact: SACRED, INVIOLABLE"; (2) "banned on grounds of morality or taste or as constituting

a risk: outlawed by common consent: DISAPPROVED, PRO-
SCRIBED."

Is *fuck* taboo because it is sacred, venerable, and charged
with supernatural power? Or is it outlawed by common
consent, immoral, and proscribed? The short answer is:
nobody knows, though, as we shall see, there are more than
a few learned opinions. Henry Miller had the vulgarian's-
eye view of the world and concluded that the why of the
taboo was unknown, but the raw force and danger of the
words were indisputable:

> What is unutterable is *fuck* and *cunt,* pure and
> simple, they must only be mentioned in limited
> editions; otherwise, the world would be shat-
> tered into pieces. Bitter experience has taught
> me what supports the world is sexual relations.
> But, the real *fuck,* the real *cunt* seems to contain
> an unidentified element which is more danger-
> ous than nitroglycerine. [*Tropic of Capricorn,*
> 1939]

One may turn blue arguing that spoken words consist of
nothing but compressed air passing over the vocal cords,
across the tongue, and through the lips—sounds, noises
even—but human beings in almost every society tend to
select a few of these sounds and set them aside for that
special fearful thrill and sacred fear.

As James McDonald observed in the introduction to his
Dictionary of Obscenity, Taboo and Euphemism:

> Our Germanic ancestors avoided words for par-
> ticularly fearsome animals. Their word for a
> bear, for example, is unknown because it was
> never recorded, though from philological evi-
> dence we can be reasonably certain that such a
> word existed. *Bear* is itself a euphemism for this
> missing word: it means "the brown one." So too
> in Anglo-Saxon times, when death was an ever-
> present threat, the ancestor of the modern word
> *die* was taboo. It was written down for the first
> time only after the Norman Conquest.

In parts of West Africa, the word for "snake" is never
used; instead the reptile is referred to euphemistically as
"the stick we saw this morning" or "that piece of rope that
killed our chicken." In other parts of the world, the names
of certain ancestors or blood relatives may never be uttered.
The Hebrews never allowed God's name to pass their lips,
and many Orthodox Jews still will not write the Name. The
saying "Speak of the devil" comes from the belief that if
you spoke Satan's name he would promptly answer the
summons.

In *The Golden Bough*, Sir James Frazer goes on at some
length listing cultures and peoples and the words they may
not speak. Frequently, the names of kings and emperors
were kept secret, held sacred, forbidden, banished from the
language. And if the new royal name sounded like other
known words, the language itself had to be changed. In
many cultures a man may not pronounce the name of his

mother-in-law, or a woman may not pronounce—even mentally!—the names of her father-in-law or brothers-in-law. As Frazer pointed out, it is as if the "savage" is unable to distinguish between words and objects. And as Ariel Arango, a dirty-word psychoanalyst and author of *Dirty Words: Psychoanalytic Insights,* observed, "It would be as if during Prohibition in the United States, not only the sale of whisky had been forbidden but the reading of the bottle labels in a loud voice as well."

Instead of fearing and worshipping bears, snakes, Yahweh, kings, violence, or their mothers-in-law, Americans used to get their fearful and sacred thrills from sex and excretion. As Read observed, "The psychological motivation for taboo lies deep, and probably has its root in the fear of the mysterious power of the sex impulse."

Thus Read was one of the first to argue that dirty words were created for the purpose of giving scandal:

> The ordinary reaction to a display of filth and vulgarity should be a neutral one or else disgust; but the reaction to certain words connected with excrement and sex is neither of these, but a titillating thrill of scandalized perturbation. Such a word . . . is endowed by the hearers with mysterious and uncanny meanings; it chills the blood and raises gooseflesh.

In short, Read concluded, "Obscenity is an artificially created product . . . a small group of words which function as 'obscenity symbols,' and all virtuous people tacitly enter into a conspiracy to maintain the sacredness of these symbols." If dirty words did not exist we would invent them because they "perform a function for speakers of standard English by serving as scapegoats, ministering to the deep-rooted need for symbols of the forbidden. They canalize a certain emotion and thus leave the remainder of the language free from it."

More recently, one detects this same "canalization" at work in the modern valence of so-called hate-speech words, in which one is forbidden to utter slurs or epithets based on a growing list that currently includes race, sex, ethnic origin, disability, religion, or sexual orientation. As Robert Hughes observed in *The Culture of Complaint,* while discussing the current zealotry for political correctness: "We want to create a sort of linguistic Lourdes, where evil and misfortune are dispelled by a dip in the waters of euphemism."

Scholars have argued at considerable length that words are words, and the f-word is only a word, because it's not what it *means* that bothers people. Sexual intercourse, copulation, making the beast with two backs, and heterosexual reproduction all mean almost exactly the same thing, but unlike those other expressions, the f-word plays upon our sensibilities like a meat cleaver scoring a harpsichord. It's vulgar, that's all, because we have made it so. The same is true of *nigger,* which was once overwhelmingly preferred to *black,* because *black* was heavily tabooed and extremely offensive, a proscription that did not evaporate until the

Black Power movement of the 1960s. "To a linguist," observed Steven Pinker in a *New York Times* editorial (April 5, 1994), "the phenomenon is familiar: the euphemism treadmill. People invent new 'polite' words to refer to emotionally laden or distasteful things, but the euphemism becomes tainted by association and the new one that must be found acquires its own negative connotations." What else could possibly explain how often the sanctioned term is a near synonym of the offensive one: "people of color" instead of "colored people," "African-American" instead of "Afro-American"?

Perhaps, as Read suggests, we carefully and subconsciously gather all the indelicate and unseemly associations we have with the brute act of reproduction, incest, sex outside marriage, sex without love, selfish sex, child sexual abuse, fatal venereal diseases—and assign them all to a single unspeakable word. When the word is uttered, it stirs up all these unconscious, unspeakable aspects of sexual congress, which we don't like to think about because they threaten the social order in a terrifying way.

Fuck may have held sway for several centuries as the most terrifying word in public discourse, but, as we saw, it is rapidly being replaced by *nigger,* now contending with *cunt* for Most Unutterable status. If we first must gather all the social ugliness we find and load it onto the chosen word, there's still plenty of ugliness out there to be rounded up and heaped onto the n-word. Historical memories of slavery, lynchings, brute dehumanization, and invidious hatred based on race are all temporarily displaced and discharged by sending the word *nigger* out of the village like a tormented goat . . . and the village celebrates afterward, until another word is needed, and the lottery is drawn.

And you thought you were only cussing!

After Read's groundbreaking article, nothing much happened until 1954, when Dr. Leo Stone wrote "On the Principal Obscene Word of the English Language." If Freud was the father of psychoanalysis, Leo Stone was the stepfather of the dirtiest word. He adopted it after it turned up repeatedly during therapy in the reveries of a fascinating patient.

The occasion for Stone's article was what he carefully avoided admitting might be an enviable clinical experience. Stone had a female patient who said, during sudden pauses in her free association, the phrase "I want to fuck the analyst" would come into her mind. In the spirit of the disinterested scientist, Stone dutifully wrote: "It should be noted that the patient was an attractive woman, thoroughly feminine in appearance and overt behavior . . . definitely careful, almost precious, in her choice of words and in her accent." Once, after therapy was over, the beautiful woman paused at the door and said, "Now the phrase comes to me—'I want to rape the analyst.' "

Dr. Stone didn't quite know what to make of the woman's disorder, so he created a 25-page scholarly article featuring 109 footnotes, thoroughly tracing the etymology of *fuck*, cataloguing linguistic and philological theories on the subject, and speculating about *fuck*'s powerful psychoanalytic implications. Talk about sublimation and displacement! Stone wanted to know everything he could about the word and the peculiar pleasure his patient took in uttering it. In the process, he compiled an encyclopedic treatise on the dirtiest word, and—one can only hope—discovered just what was on his patient's mind.

Stone's diagnosis:

> The patient's use of this "dirty" word, especially in its paradoxical aggressive direction, was in the anal sphere of her sexuality, which permitted every inference of severe early training—in the character of management of aggression or emotional display in connection with money, in the actual sphere of dirt and cleanliness, in her ritualistic toilet habits, in a few early memories, and in many manifest dreams regarding the excretory functions. This verbal displacement of excretory impulses has justly been accorded an important place in the general problem of pleasure in obscene language.

Because we owe psychoanalysts so much for their forward-looking treatises on the subject and for their early appreciation of the splendor and mystery of dirty words, I am loath to say anything bad about them, but even the casual reader will apprehend that these fellows were more than a tad warped themselves. Listen to this:

> Insofar as obvious aggression is implicit in the words, one thinks of the aggression of original

> oral deprivation . . . the sensations originating in the development of teeth as connected with primordial phallic sexual attitudes would be relevant to this hypothesis, as it is to the well-known castration and masturbatory symbolism of teeth in dreams. The interference with sucking ascribed to eruption of teeth was mentioned early by Freud and Abraham. Ferenczi stated strongly the conception of the tooth as "Ur-penis."

Of course! The scales fall away from your eyes! The tooth is an "Ur-penis," and the tooth fairy is gay. It makes perfect sense!

As Stone continued his analysis of this admittedly fascinating patient, he discovered something he described as "crucial and especially challenging to me," namely, "the patient's receptive oral wishes, i.e., with her impulse to *suck* [Stone's emphasis]." He observed that the patient took "pleasure in having her husband suck her breast as part of the fore-pleasure . . . the occasional fleeting wish for fellatio or cunnilingus, or both, during intercourse."

We don't need a psychiatrist to ascertain just how disturbed she was, and if these repulsive tendencies and deviant wishes were not filtered through Stone's disinterested, clinical descriptions, the reader would most likely fling the article aside in disgust. It's only the word-lover's fascination that allows us to persevere.

Stone cited a study observing that male infants in states

of frustration and rage at the breast frequently develop erections. Thus in the deepest layers of experience there is a relationship between a *disturbance* of sucking and the physiological corollary of the impulse to "fuck."

After careful examination of the patient and an even closer examination of the dirtiest word, Stone "developed the preliminary idea that the rhyme with the word 'suck' may have been an important unconscious determinant in the linguistic fixation and taboo of our word in general usage, regardless of its origin."

OK, I guess . . . Yes, I'm beginning to see that he is onto something. The staying power and taboo of the f-word derives from the fact that it rhymes with *suck*. This would also explain why the twin imprecations of *cocksucker* and *motherfucker* end up together in the same sentence when someone is especially displeased.

If we walked into a working-class tavern, told the patrons that the word *fuck* had been around since at least 1500 or so, and solicited opinions from the group about why it has been so popular and prevalent for so long, one of them might opine, "Do you think it's because it rhymes with *suck*?" But the same sentiment coming from a learned psychoanalyst sounds like this:

> I believe that some linguistic evidence reflexively supports the conception of the enduring dynamic importance of the pregenital organizations in adult sexuality. Of the series "active-passive, phallic-castrated, masculine-feminine,"

it would be reasonable to assume that all find some representation in the putative linguistic transition from "suck" to "fuck."

There is a possibility that, if not in the demonstrable outer phenomenology of linguistic history, there is a latent psychological relation between the words "fuck" and "suck" deeply antecedent to the perfect rhyme between the words.

Stone seems to be saying that we take pleasure in obscene language because we are verbally displacing excretory impulses, which would otherwise manifest themselves in chronic, panpsychic dysentery. Instead of offering to shit on our neighbor's head, we call him a shithead. Instead of the unbearable thought that our mothers actually fucked someone before we were born, we project our revulsion for this truth onto others by calling them motherfuckers. But it's not communication we're after so much as purgation or emesis, as we've noted before:

That autistic (specifically auto-erotic) anality contributes to the peculiar effect of basic obscene words, entirely aside from the association with primitive emissive relief, is my conviction. The pleasure in uttering obscene words lies not only in the communicative effect on the object but in the simultaneous autistic pleasure of utterance.

Psychoanalysts are as nervous about censuring speech as lawyers are: speech is a tool of both their trades. Psychoanalysts encourage, even insist that, their patients use the dirty words, because in the words of Norman O. Brown:

> Psychoanalysis, of course, must regard language as a repository of the psychic history of mankind, and the exploration of words, by wit or poetry or scientific etymology, as one of the avenues into the unconscious. [*Life Against Death* (paraphrasing Freud and Ferenczi)]

The sex and excrement terms are especially important, because the two are easily confused in the deep recesses of the obsessional neurotic. This theme runs through all of literature and has caused more trouble for authors who dare to write about it than all the political tracts ever written. You couldn't buy a copy of D. H. Lawrence's *Lady Chatterley's Lover* for decades for just this reason. Instead of quoting the dirty passages for the modern reader who thinks nothing of them after having the misfortune of reading Judith Krantz, it's more enlightening to hear Lawrence's views in the nonfictional format:

> The sex functions and the excrementory functions in the human body work so close together, yet they are, so to speak, utterly different in direction. Sex is a creative flow, the excrementory flow is towards dissolution, decreation, if

we may use such a word. In the really healthy human being the distinction between the two is instant; our profoundest instincts are perhaps our instincts of opposition between the two flows. But in the degraded human being the deep instincts have gone dead, and then the two flows become identical. *This* is the secret of really vulgar and of pornographic people: the sex flow and the excrement flow is the same thing to them. ["Pornography and Obscenity," *Criterion Miscellany* 5, London, 1929]

In Kelly Anspaugh's essay "Powers of Ordure: James Joyce and the Excremental Vision(s)," recently published in *Mosaic,* the author neatly juxtaposes Freud's observations about obsessional neurotics with Joyce's anal fantasies expressed in letters to his wife. First Freud: "We can observe the result of a regressive deterioration of the genital organization: all the phantasies originally conceived on the genital level are set back on to the anal level; the penis is replaced by the faecal mass, the vagina by the rectum."

Then Joyce: "Fuck me if you can squatting in the closet, with our clothes up, grunting like a young sow doing her dung, and a big fat dirty thing snaking out of your backside."

I was all for free speech and against censorship, until I read that passage. Now, I want to ban James Joyce's letters. They are just too much! I want to go hole up in that tavern we just visited and bask in the good cheer and vulgar epithets of my fellow citizens, so I can watch the game on TV and forget about what all the perceptive authors and learned experts have to say about just why I swear so much.

In *Dirty Words,* a fascinating compendium of mythology, psychology, anthropology, and any other *-ology* that has ever turned its sights on the subject of dirty words, Arango, another M.D., seconds the notion that dirty words are required in free association:

> The findings of psychoanalysis leave no doubt about the legitimacy of this requirement. In obscene language the very essence of our being is revealed, the *ipsa hominis essentia.* With it the mysterious and eternal instincts are expressed in their most pure and transparent form, without veils and modesty.

For non-Latin scholars, *ipsa hominis essentia* means "the thing inside of us that makes us want to scream 'Fuck!' in a crowded theater." And for nonlegal scholars who are complacent about the recent movements to annihilate free speech in the name of civil rights, take note that such an agenda involves a lot more than banning sexual innuendo.

The Rules of Engagement

One man's vulgarity is another's lyric.

—Justice John Harlan, *Cohen v. California*

When and where may you swear? No easy answer there, because the question is a legal one, and unless you pay extra for a one-handed lawyer, the advice you receive will be ambiguous, because it will usually begin with "On the one hand . . ." and end with "On the other hand . . ."

Worse yet, using dirty words almost always poses First Amendment problems. Law students spend the better part of three years beetling their brows over the study of constitutional law, discovering to their initial horror a mercurial, opaque, highly theoretical system of textual exegesis, which nobody but the tenured and long-winded professor pretends to understand. This horror promptly vanishes once the bar exam is passed, and the young lawyer realizes that the practice of law is rife with constitutional issues, which can only be resolved by hundreds of billable hours of research and writing.

And the capsheaf of con-law contwistification is First Amendment law. The First Amendment protects "freedom of speech" and has spawned an absorbing delusional system of case law, because the harder you work to understand it, the more complex and inscrutable it becomes, until its tracts and tiers of analyses, its time, place, and manner restrictions, its public and private figures and forums, its symbolic expressions and invasions of privacy—all evanesce into vaporous metaphysics.

When it comes to freedom of expression, the class may as well be team-taught by Confucius and Immanuel Kant. And that's at the schooling stage! When a First Amendment problem falls into the hands of real lawyers and judges, every learned orifice within a billable hour of the case erupts in ideological incontinence: the verbal diarrhea, the sophistical spew fills conference rooms, courtrooms, and judges' chambers. Just mention the possibility of a First Amendment issue and fifty-page briefs appear like flies from seething maggots. The keyboards of clerks and associates spring to life, clattering forth deliberative periods bedecked with four independent phrases and eight dependent clauses. The cataracts of print inspired by the freedom of expression fill tracts and textbooks, law-review articles and federal court opinions.

The legal profession adores speech—worships it! The First Amendment protects the livelihood of those who venerate it—and if it protects profanity and swearing as well, so be it, for practitioners of swearing, of magic, and of the law all use oaths, incantations, and I-do-solemnly-swears to work their sorcery. But the best kind of speech is not free, it's the kind you charge for by the hour. Shakespeare said the breath of an unfee'd lawyer amounts to nothing. Just add a retainer with an hourly fee schedule, and the effluent acquires the specific gravity of blackstrap molasses and bullshit.

The inquiring vulgarian with four spare lifetimes and a burning desire to find out whether he may legally scream "Fuck!" in a crowded theater will come away in confusion if he looks for his answer in the opinions of the United States Supreme Court. Instead of an understanding of free speech, the reader will acquire manifest strabismus and an allergic reaction to the passive voice; he will be sucked into a maelstrom of circumlocution, buffeted by the flotsam of seven-syllable Latin derivatives and the jetsam of Old English rubrics deriving from feudal common law.

The first two amendments to the Constitution show that this country was founded by hale and hearty fellows who liked to cuss and shoot guns. The First Amendment says, "Congress shall make no law . . . abridging the freedom of speech." The wording is extremely important. The language does not confer a right of free speaking on citizens, rather it presumes this right and makes it illegal for Congress to make laws restricting it. The founding fathers (and some of the mothers) were rabble-rousers—they were already contentedly cussing at governments whenever the spirit moved them, and they wanted to be sure no government of their creation was going to pass any laws against people speaking freely.

Most speech (with a few notable exceptions) is protected from being abridged by federal, state, or local governments trying to protect the tender sensibilities of people who don't want to hear it. The U.S. Supreme Court has repeatedly insisted that "if there is a bedrock principle underlying the First Amendment, it is that the government may not prohibit the expression of an idea simply because society finds the idea itself offensive or disagreeable." When it comes to protecting the citizenry from false ideas, such as "niggers are dumb," or offensive speech, such as "men are fucking animals," the Supreme Court has tended to side with guys like Nietzsche, who observed that the truth is not such an innocuous or incompetent creature as to require protection.

Because of this principle, American Nazis were allowed to march through the predominantly Jewish community of Skokie, Illinois; wild-eyed radicals can burn flags on the courthouse steps; and a guy with a bad attitude can walk into a courtroom wearing a jacket emblazoned with the words "FUCK THE DRAFT." Nobody has ever changed the wording of the First Amendment, but—along with the rest of the Constitution—it means something slightly different every time a new justice arrives to warm the bench.

For our purposes, the dedicated vulgarian should know that currently there are at least five categories of "unprotected" speech—that is, speech not protected by the First

Amendment. Never mind that the First Amendment itself makes no such distinction. Some speech is "protected" and some is "unprotected" because—well—because the Supreme Court found some speech that it wanted to ban, and so it said, "Henceforth this speech shall be known as 'unprotected' speech." When the Court calls speech "unprotected" it means governments may ban it if they want to and arrest you for using it, or even allow others to sue you.

The five main categories of unprotected speech are: (1) fraudulent misrepresentation; (2) defamation; (3) advocacy of imminent lawless behavior; (4) "fighting words" addressed to a particular person or group and designed to incite them to immediate violence; (5) obscenity.

Vulgarity, profanity, obscenity, and indecency are often fungible to the layperson. The Supreme Court also uses them interchangeably, with the single, important exception of obscenity. *Obscenity* is a magic word that opens like a Chinese box containing other magic Chinese boxes.

When the government hauls someone into court on an obscenity charge, the Supreme Court currently uses the three-prong test from *Miller* v. *California* (1973), each prong of which must be met, to determine if the stuff is obscene:

> (1) The "average person, applying contemporary community standards would find that the work, taken as a whole, appeals to the prurient interest";

(2) The work "depicts or describes, in a patently offensive way, sexual conduct specifically defined by the applicable state law"; and

(3) The work, taken as a whole, lacks "serious literary, artistic, political, or scientific value."

Don't bother remembering any of it, because there were four dissenting justices in the case, which means we will be getting a new test any day now. Decades of litigation have assigned specialized meaning to each word and phrase, from "average person" to "taken as a whole" to "sexual conduct." But perhaps the most important word is *prurient,* which would melt your computer's chip if you used it as a search term on Westlaw (the most powerful computerized legal database) because it would retrieve eight billion cases.

Prurient means "having a tendency to excite lustful thoughts." Now you know why it is so popular. Twelve years and thousands of federal lawsuits after *Miller,* the Court modified this definition of *prurient* to exclude works that, although they "excite lustful thoughts," provoke "only normal, healthy sexual desires" (*Brockett* v. *Spokane Arcades,* 1985). After a few more decades of litigation, we'll receive a pronouncement from above about what is "normal" and "healthy" and how many hours of sleep we should be getting each night. Justice Potter Stewart once cut to the chase and gave up wrestling with the unworkable onion of tunicate obscenity definitions by observing, "I know it when I see it."

If you are sued or arrested for swearing, or for using offensive speech somewhere outside the workplace, you'll most likely be charged under a statute banning "fighting words" (disturbing the peace) or obscenity. If you can afford a trip through the federal court system, you will win, and the government will lose, unless you were openly and obviously inciting a particular person or a particular group of persons to immediate violence.

Just ask 2 Live Crew. These rap musicians and artists, struggling to express truth in the poetic vernacular of the streets, have been arrested, jailed, prosecuted, and sued from hell to breakfast. Every time the government hauls them into court, the disgusting vulgarians win and the government loses, because the bad-boy rappers are protected by the First Amendment. On top of that, the attendant publicity drives their filthy albums straight up the pop charts and they make millions overnight. Then they go on to make new songs about their would-be tormentors, in which the group chants over and over that the sheriff of Broward County, Florida, and the governor of Florida "suck dick," and their wives "eat pussy." One can almost hear government officials begging law enforcement officers *not* to arrest rap musicians, because the prosecutors don't want to hear another hit single about how they had their asses kicked in the federal court of appeals.

Because of the well-established "prurient" requirement, foul language and profanity are almost never considered obscene, because, as we saw earlier, they are acts of hostility and aggression, not prurience. When N.W.A. sings "Fuck tha Police," an average citizen applying contemporary community standards will not be "excited to lustful thoughts." Keep these five categories in mind while we sample some Supreme Court cases important to vulgar speech.

Tenured legal scholars get lost in the diffuse and complex hermeneutics of First Amendment theory, because they have no unifying perspective from which to view the proliferating themes, the tracks and tiers of scrutiny and analyses featured in the orotund opinions of the Supreme Court. We shall avoid going astray by following the spoor left by our favorite single-syllable word. Instead of a clew of thread in the labyrinth of First Amendment law, we will follow the trail left by the f-word—a one-legged goat whose hoofprints appear like divots, nicks, defects in the otherwise august majesty of the constitutional landscape. The dirty word has clopped through just over twenty years of Supreme Court jurisprudence, and every time it appears, it's usually because the government is trying to regulate the time, place, or manner in which an honest citizen may stand on a chair and say, "Fuck you!"

For a quick tour of First Amendment law (guided by our goatish uniped), boot up your computer, plug in your modem, dial up and log on to Westlaw. You will be asked to select a database. You should choose "SCT" for the database containing all the U.S. Supreme Court cases ever published. When instructed to "PLEASE FORMULATE YOUR SEARCH TERMS OR QUERY," put on your afternoon-of-a-faun costume, grab a set of pan pipes and a grape-stained Methuselah of pastoral wine, and type "FUCK" at the prompt. "PLEASE WAIT," the software will advise, and four seconds later the screen will display a list of every Supreme Court opinion containing the second-dirtiest word. In February 1996, there were nine such opinions, beginning with the 1971 case of *Cohen v. California* and ending with the 1993 case of *Wisconsin v. Mitchell.*

What does this say about the moral decay of Western Civilization? The opinions of the Supreme Court fill more than five hundred volumes containing 191 years of jurisprudence running from *Marbury v. Madison* in 1803 to the softbound volumes of the Court's most recent opinions. *Fuck* does not appear until 1971, in volume 403, 168 years after *Marbury.* If the history of American constitutional law were a twenty-four-hour day, *fuck* would appear at 9:28 in the evening (on Saturday night, after everybody in the house was drunk and in bed with somebody else's spouse).

For 168 years, the Court did everything in its power to avoid the f-word—ignored it, deleted it, employed euphemisms, dashes, asterisks, anything but printing the thing in its Spartan vulgarity. Now, here at the end of the twentieth century, *fuck* is simply unavoidable. The justices of the Supreme Court—including at least one person who was almost disqualified for saying things such as "pubic hair" and for having *Playboy* magazines in his bachelor apartment—now are compelled by modern depravity to print the f-word in their own opinions. The word has become so essential to the deranged psyche of contemporary man that even the

Supreme Court *must* use it! As Hugh Rawson observed in *Wicked Words:* "It [*fuck*] is the prototypical example of the close, not to say intimate, connection between sex and violence in our culture, and it also provides a litmus test of society's controls over sexual expression"—precisely the reason it also provides a litmus test for government efforts to suppress speech.

Two of the nine cases had nothing to do with the First Amendment and feature the f-word only as an incidental threat or expletive. The remaining seven cases present the following thorny, f-word conundrums for the nine Philosopher Kings and Queens in black gowns:

(1) COHEN V. CALIFORNIA (1971). In 1968, Paul Robert Cohen walked into a California courthouse wearing a jacket bearing the words "FUCK THE DRAFT," which were plainly visible. He was arrested for violating section 415 of the California Penal Code, which prohibits "maliciously and willfully disturb[ing] the peace or quiet of any neighborhood or person . . . by offensive conduct."

The U.S. Supreme Court struck down the California ordinance: "Absent a more particularized and compelling reason for its actions, the State may not . . . make the simple public display of this single four-letter expletive a criminal offense." The case features Justice John Harlan's oft-quoted observation that "while the particular four-letter word being litigated here is perhaps more distasteful than most others of its genre, it is nevertheless often true that one man's vulgarity is another's lyric."

(2) HESS V. INDIANA (1973). A campus antiwar demonstration in Bloomington, Indiana, ended when the sheriff and his deputies began moving demonstrators out of the street. Without addressing any particular person or group, defendant Gregory Hess said, "We'll take the fucking street later." The sheriff arrested Hess for disorderly conduct, a charge the Indiana Supreme Court upheld.

The U.S. Supreme Court reversed, holding that the defendant's statement was not "obscene," did not consist of "fighting words," did not have "a tendency to lead to violence," and was "nothing more than advocacy of illegal action at some indefinite future time," all of which meant that Hess's statement was protected by the First Amendment and he should not have been arrested for disorderly conduct.

Note the familiar words and phrases in quotes above— they are terms of art and legal incantations, which the Court (like *Alice in Wonderland*) uses to cast spells on the speech at issue, magically transforming it into an expression that is either "protected" or "unprotected" by the First Amendment, if for no other reason than that the Court says it shall be so.

(3) SOUTHEASTERN PROMOTIONS V. CONRAD (1975). A promoter applied to the Chattanooga, Tennessee, municipal board for permission to perform the rock musical *Hair*. The municipal board concluded that the production would not be "in the best interest of the community." The promoter sought an injunction permitting it to use the auditorium.

Ruling in favor of the municipal board, the federal district court and the court of appeals dismissed the promoter's complaint.

The Supreme Court reversed, holding that denying use of the municipal facilities constituted a "prior restraint" and came dangerously close to outright censorship. The f-word would never have appeared in the Court's opinion were it not for the concurring and dissenting justices who appended various district court exhibits containing excerpts from the script of *Hair*.

In an effort to show the vulgar nature of the play, the district court had catalogued samples of "street language" and "repeated use of the word 'fuck,' " from the play:

> BERGER: I hate the fuckin' world, don't you?
> CLAUDE: I hate the fuckin' world, I hate the fuckin' winter, I hate these fuckin' streets.
> BERGER: I wish the fuck it would snow at least. . . .
> CLAUDE: Oh, fuck!
> BERGER: Oh, fucky, fuck, fuck!

Pretty dangerous stuff, you must admit.

Justice William Brennan concurred with the majority's opinion for different reasons. He took the multicultural view—which is now being used in lower federal courts to protect the lyrics of rap musicians—that words such as *fuck* and *bullshit* are not considered obscene or vulgar in black vernacular, and at least some of the characters, including Claude, were young African-Americans:

> Today's decision will thus have its greatest impact on broadcasters desiring to reach, and listening audiences composed of, persons who do not share the Court's view as to which words or expressions are acceptable and who, for a variety of reasons, including a conscious desire to flout majoritarian conventions, express themselves using words that may be regarded as offensive by those from different socio-economic backgrounds. In this context, the Court's decision may be seen for what, in the broader perspective, it really is: another of the dominant culture's inevitable efforts to force those groups who do not share its mores to conform to its way of thinking, acting, and speaking.

These days the "dominant" culture is one that abhors discrimination and sexual harassment more than almost any other evils, and one wonders if the Court would show equal lenience to a promoter who wanted to put on a play prominently featuring a positive-outcome rape scenario, or the tabooed n-word used in a hateful manner by white actors who don't get killed or put in jail for their verbal crimes before the play ends.

So far, so good for offensive vulgarians. But then the

Supreme Court rendered the most dangerous First Amendment case of all.

(4) FEDERAL COMMUNICATIONS COMMISSION V. PACIFICA FOUNDATION (1978). Early one weekday afternoon in New York City, listener-supported radio station WBAI broadcast George Carlin's famous seven-dirty-words monologue, about words "you definitely wouldn't ever say ever" on the air: "shit, piss, fuck, cunt, cocksucker, motherfucker, and tits." The monologue was part of a program about attitudes toward language.

Responding to a complaint from a single motorist, the FCC determined that the monologue was indecent and prohibited by statutes written by—guess who?—the FCC. The Supreme Court agreed with the FCC's disinterested determination that the monologue was "indecent," but the Court could not reach an agreement on the constitutional rationale for its decision (probably because it was the wrong decision).

Speech had never been legally banned because it was "indecent," and the seven-dirty-words monologue did not fit into any other known category of unprotected speech, i.e., it was not obscene (because it was not prurient), it did not consist of fighting words, it did not advocate imminent illegal conduct, it was not defamatory, and so on. It was simply offensive, which readers will recall was insufficient to keep the Nazis out of Skokie, Illinois.

Before this case, the Supreme Court occasionally had upheld zoning ordinances regulating (but not banning) adult theaters and bookstores because of secondary effects, such as low property values and high crime rates, but *FCC v. Pacifica* was the first instance in which the Court upheld an ordinance aimed directly at speech itself. Gerald Gunther, author of *Constitutional Law* (12th ed., 1991), the textbook used by most law students, called the *Pacifica* case "startlingly bad news" (p. 1163), because it was the first time in the history of the United States that there was "majority support [on the Court] of a prohibition of speech because it is offensive to the audience."

(5) BOARD OF EDUCATION V. PICO (1982). The Board of Education for several school districts in New York ordered nine books to be removed from its high school and junior high school libraries. The books had appeared on a list published by a conservative parents' group, and the board ordered them removed because they were "anti-American, anti-Christian, anti-Semitic, and just plain filthy."

The f-word came into the opinion again by way of a dissenting justice (Lewis Powell) who added an appendix featuring "excerpts which led the Board to look into the educational suitability of the books in question." If you seek out the full opinion and read the appendix in its entirety, don't say I didn't warn you. READER DISCRETION IS ADVISED. It contains some of the most offensively racist, sexist, and just plain filthy language I've ever seen. Lucky for me, I have only to feature the sentences containing *fuck* to complete this empirical undertaking, and the f-word is by far the least offensive part of this catalogue. If anyone is offended by the comparatively tame excerpts found here, blame Justice Powell or the authors themselves, not me.

Four of the nine books did not feature the f-word and were offensive for other reasons. The other five, and their accompanying goat spoors, are as follows:

Soul on Ice, Eldridge Cleaver, pages 157–58: "There are white men who will pay you to fuck their wives. They approach you and say, 'How would you like to fuck a white woman?' "

A Hero Ain't Nothing but a Sandwich, Alice Childress, page 10: "Fuck the society"; pages 64–65: "The hell with the junkie, the wino, the capitalist, the welfare checks, the world . . . yeah, and fuck you too! They can have back the spread and curtains, I'm too old for them fuckin bunnies anyway."

The Fixer, Bernard Malamud, page 52: "What do you think goes on in the wagon at night: Are the drivers on their knees fucking their mothers?"; page 90: "Fuck yourself, said the blinker, etc."; page 189: "Also there's a lot of fucking in the Old Testament, so how is that religious?"; page 192: "You better go fuck yourself, Bok, said Kogin, I'm onto your Jew tricks."

Go Ask Alice, anonymous, page 110: "You fucking miss Polly pure"; page 117: "Then he said that all I needed was a good fuck."

Slaughterhouse Five, Kurt Vonnegut, Jr., page 29: " 'Get out of the road, you dumb motherfucker.' The last word was still a novelty in the speech of white people in 1944. It was fresh and astonishing to Billy, who had never fucked anybody"; page 120: "Why don't you go fuck yourself? Don't think I haven't tried . . . he was going to have revenge, and that revenge was sweet. . . . It's the sweetest thing there is, said Lazzaro. People fuck with me, he said, and Jesus Christ are they ever fucking sorry"; page 134: "Oh, I'll never fuck a Polack any more."

Believe it or not, the U.S. Supreme Court sent the case back for trial, because, although it found that the board had the power to remove books from the library, this removal must not be carried out in a "narrowly partisan or political manner," which would deny student access to ideas with which the authorities disagree. The case was largely proce- dural, for the Court went out of its way to explain that there were plenty of valid grounds for removal, including "educational suitability," which the board had failed to ar- ticulate properly. More important, the Court took pains to point out that it was saying nothing about the power of school authorities to *add* (or not add) books to the library, broadly hinting that the whole case could have been avoided if the board had simply not stocked the books in the first place, and then kept an appropriate explanation handy to rebut any challenge.

As we will see later, the First Amendment applies with considerably reduced force in schools and in the workplace.

(6)   MASSON V. *NEW YORKER* MAGAZINE   (1991).   The fa- mous case of alleged defamation arising out of allegedly altered quotations, and one of the longest disputes since *Jarndyce* v. *Jarndyce* in Dickens's *Bleak House.* The plaintiff,

Jeffrey Masson, a noted psychoanalyst, quotes himself as saying, " 'Fuck you,' I said, 'why should I do that?' " Masson was unhappy with the way journalist Janet Malcom had quoted him in an article published in *The New Yorker*. The litigation dealt with some thorny defamation issues, but otherwise offers almost no instruction on the First Amendment implications of the f-word.

However, the abiding, energetic, and expensive vindictiveness of the plaintiff does offer a few vivid lessons on why litigation is almost always the last and worst alternative in a running dispute. The case lasted almost ten years, went to the court of appeals twice, then to the Supreme Court, then back to trial, with legal meters running the whole time. It perfectly illustrates Ambrose Bierce's definition of a lawsuit as "a machine which you go into as a pig and come out of as a sausage." Asking who won is the wrong question, as Voltaire well knew: "I was never ruined but twice: once when I lost a lawsuit, and once when I won one." But above all, the dispute provides a case study of Gore Vidal's trenchant observation that "for certain people, after fifty, litigation takes the place of sex."

(7) WISCONSIN V. MITCHELL (1993). The case shows once again how the sword of legislation aimed at discrimination, hate crimes, or hate speech and designed to protect minorities is a double-edged one. On October 7, 1989, a group of young black men and boys, including the defendant, Todd Mitchell, gathered at an apartment complex in Kenosha, Wisconsin. The group discussed a scene from the

motion picture *Mississippi Burning,* in which a white man beat a young black boy who was praying.

When the group moved outside, Mitchell asked them, "Do you all feel hyped up to move on some white people?" Soon the group spotted a young white boy walking on the other side of the street. Mitchell then said, "You all want to fuck somebody up? There goes a white boy; go get him."

The group beat the boy unconscious and stole his tennis shoes. He was in a coma for four days.

A jury convicted Mitchell of aggravated battery, which ordinarily carries a maximum sentence of two years' imprisonment. But because the jury also found that Mitchell had intentionally selected his victim because of the boy's race, the maximum sentence was increased to seven years under Wisconsin's enhancement-of-penalty statute, which kicks in whenever the defendant "intentionally selects the person against whom the crime ... is committed ... because of the race, religion, color, disability, sexual orientation, national origin or ancestry of that person." Mitchell was ultimately sentenced to four years, double the normal maximum.

Mitchell's lawyers argued that the Wisconsin statute in effect punished bigoted or offensive thought and therefore violated the First Amendment. And what would happen, asked the lawyers, if somebody committed a felony against a member of a protected group and the court used bigoted speech or opinions that had been expressed years before the event to prove discriminatory motive? The Wisconsin Supreme Court bought this argument and said that the statute unconstitutionally punished the "subjective mental process" of selecting a victim because of his protected status.

In a unanimous opinion, the U.S. Supreme Court reversed, holding that the statute punished motive, not speech, and nothing more, and that trial judges often take motive into account when sentencing anyway. The fear that bigoted beliefs would be used as evidence in a subsequent criminal trial was "too speculative."

Given the wording of the statute and nature of the crime, the decision was correct. But the idiosyncratic preferences contained in such well-meaning legislation become clear if one imagines Mitchell saying, "Do you all feel hyped up to move on some infants? There goes an infant; go get him," or, "Do you all feel hyped up to move on some ugly, fat people and some little old folks?" and so on. In which case, Mitchell would be serving two years for battery instead of four.

Thus concludes the goatish tour of First Amendment law. Note how the f-word provides a concrete talisman for knocking our sticks against in the ethereal forests of First Amendment law. This tawdry and vulgar epithet has sustained us on our journey through the conceptual netherworlds in much the same way the vision of Beatrice kept Dante going on his tour through the underworld. In the next century, laws against saying "fuck" will probably be anachronisms. The word scholar with a childlike curiosity about how the government is attacking speech and policing thought will need to use a racist slur or sexist epithet to conduct a similar survey.

Cohen and *Pacifica* are the two most important cases for vulgarians. They illustrate a typical government tactic in First Amendment litigation.

Explain the facts of *Cohen* to any second-grade class, and they'll tell you that the government arrested Cohen to punish him for using a bad word and for saying something bad about the draft. Civil libertarians and linguists know that the two are inseparable. The government knew that the First Amendment would not allow it to punish Cohen for his ideas or his speech, so it pretended to be concerned about the defendant's safety and keeping the peace. "No, really, your honor," said the government. "What if someone —a veteran, let's say—attacked Mr. Cohen? Or what if women and children saw the word *fuck* and couldn't look away in time?" It's true, these were the arguments.

The U.S. Supreme Court saw exactly what was up:

> Against this background, the issue flushed by this case stands out in bold relief. It is whether California can excise, as "offensive conduct," one particular scurrilous epithet from the public discourse, either upon the theory of the court below that its use is inherently likely to cause violent reaction or upon a more general asser-

> tion that the States, acting as guardians of public morality, may properly remove this offensive word from the public vocabulary.

The answer is no. A jacket proclaiming Cohen's undying love for the draft would be just as likely to provoke antagonism from draft dodgers, and somehow we know that Cohen would never have been arrested if he had written "I LOVE THE DRAFT" on his jacket. We also know that he would not have been arrested if his jacket had said simply, "I WISH THE DRAFT DID NOT EXIST BECAUSE IT'S JUST NOT FAIR," but that's a different message and a different idea than the one Cohen was after.

The lesson of *Cohen* and *FCC* v. *Pacifica* is that many people say, think, or even type on their keyboards dirty, racist, sexist, and just plain offensive words at least a dozen times a day. None of these people will have a problem, unless they use offensive speech to punctuate a seditious statement, an antiwar message, or more recently a racist or sexist stereotype, in which case their chances of being prosecuted increase exponentially. The government steadfastly will maintain throughout the litigation that it is only trying to protect public morals, children, and helpless minorities from discrimination, and that it takes no position with respect to anyone's politics, but we know better.

Radical victim-feminists in the United States and Canada at first celebrated when the Canadian Supreme Court issued its 1992 opinion in *R.* v. *Butler,* banning certain kinds of pornography because it allegedly harms women.

The Rules of Engagement

According to Jeffrey Toobin in a recent *New Yorker* article, the *Butler* opinion is being used to justify the confiscation of anything the border police consider to be pornography, including feminist political tracts and gay and lesbian erotic literature.

The U.S. Supreme Court has wisely refrained from censuring public speech or placing an outright ban on pornography, because it is almost impossible to draft and enforce statutes that define only the targeted speech. You cannot make it illegal to say "Fuck the bitch!" without also making it illegal to say "Swive the wench!" As the Court observed, again in *Cohen:*

> How is one to distinguish this from any other offensive word? Surely the State has no right to cleanse public debate to the point where it is grammatically palatable to the most squeamish among us. Yet no readily ascertainable general principle exists for stopping short of that result were we to affirm the judgment below.
>
> Indeed, we think it is largely because governmental officials cannot make principled distinctions in this area that the Constitution leaves matters of taste and style so largely to the individual.
>
> Finally, and in the same vein, we cannot indulge the facile assumption that one can forbid particular words without also running a substantial risk of suppressing ideas in the process.

> Indeed, governments might soon seize upon the censorship of particular words as a convenient guise for banning the expression of unpopular views.

Laws aimed at speech are attempts at regulating the sounds made by air passing over the human vocal cords. Imagine for a moment that the federal government passed a statute making it illegal to say "fuck" anytime, anywhere. The next day, some wiseguy would simply announce that in the light of the Supreme Court's efforts to ban free speech, the word *vuck* will be used instead of the f-word I can't say. Then he could tell the Supreme Court to go vuck itself with impunity. Unless he can be prosecuted for using a word that is 75 percent indecent, *vuck* will be perfectly legal, until the statute is amended to outlaw the word *fuck* and any combination of -*uck* preceded by a fricative consonant, including but not limited to *vuck* and *phuck*. Whereupon, the same wiseguy would simply regress to Chaucer and declare that the word *swive* will now be used in place of the f-word I can't say. And he could then tell the Supreme Court, "Swive you. Swive your mamma. Swive your little sister. Swive the nine horses you rode in on."

One has only to look at campus speech codes for laughable attempts at legislation banning specific words. The problem usually comes when the university wants to ban use of the word *nigger*, unless it is being used in a jocular manner by an African-American in a nonhostile conversation with another African-American. True PC zealots want these same prohibitions enshrined in federal statutes, in which case we will have federal courtrooms jammed to capacity with juries attentively listening to witnesses testifying about whether the n-word was used in a jocular, non-hostile manner, and whether the defendant was truly African-American if he was relatively light-skinned because one maternal grandparent was black and the other was of mixed descent—all in the interest of achieving a social order that does not discriminate on the basis of race.

Which begs the question of whether we *need* laws prohibiting racist or sexist speech. Thanks to the efforts of the entertainment industry, which never tires of showing us movies about porcine, sadistic white sheriffs and their cronies, who say "boy" every other line and like to beat up women and virtuous black people, the public has gotten the message. The overwhelming majority of the population now believes with a zeal approaching religious fervor that the only issue left regarding people who use racist or sexist speech is whether they should be shot at dawn or imprisoned for life. James Watt, Earl Butz, Al Campanis ("Jimmy The Greek"), Jimmy Breslin, Andy Rooney, Ted Danson, and most recently the historian for the House of Representatives, Christina Jeffreys, and Francis Lawrence, the president of Rutgers University, were all smothered in public opprobrium, summarily fired, or both, for making "racist" remarks—all without the help of any unconstitutional federal statute aimed at controlling their speech.

• • •

Probably the most heroic of our featured dirty-word heroes is John Wilkes—whose life proves that offensive speech is absolutely essential to freedom, and that when governments want to stifle a man's ideas, they usually do it by attacking his choice of words.

Wilkes was indirectly responsible for getting the f-word read aloud in the British Parliament during the eighteenth century. He was one of two defenders of the American colonies commemorated in the name of the town Wilkes-Barre, Pennsylvania. Bawdy limericks were responsible, at least in part, for the success of the American colonies in achieving their independence from King George III, and his dirty-word heroics provide a case study in the suppression of free speech by a tyrannical government.

Wilkes and John Montagu, fourth earl of Sandwich (from whom the sandwich takes its name), were both notoriously dissolute. Both belonged to something called the Hell Fire Club, and each had a history of pulling practical jokes on the other. According to word maven Hugh Rawson in *Wicked Words,* on one occasion, Wilkes dressed a baboon in a devil's costume, stuffed it into a trunk, and smuggled it into the club, where the earl was celebrating a Black Mass —a travesty of the Catholic mass consisting of drinking and debauchery. At the appropriate moment during the ceremonies, the "devil" was released from his trunk and hopped upon the earl's back, "scaring the bejesus out of his Lordship."

On another occasion, circa 1763, Wilkes managed one of the most famous comebacks of all time, again at the expense of the earl of Sandwich. As recorded by Sir Charles Petrie in *The Four Georges* (1935), the exchange proceeded as follows:

> THE EARL: 'Pon my honor, Wilkes, I don't
> know whether you'll die on the gallows or
> of the pox.
> WILKES: That must depend, my Lord, on
> whether I first embrace your Lordship's
> principles, or your Lordship's mistresses.

Later, Wilkes published and perhaps had a hand in composing a parody of Alexander Pope's "An Essay on Man" (1733). Pope's famous poem began with the philosophical observation:

> *. . . life can little more supply*
> *Than just to look about us and to die*

The spoof Wilkes published was entitled "An Essay on Woman." On November 15, 1763, the earl of Sandwich read it aloud to the House of Lords, beginning with the observation that

> *. . . life can little more supply*
> *Than just a few good fucks and then we die*

The House of Lords erupted in a shouting match between those who wanted the poem read and those who wanted it stopped. In *Wicked Words,* Rawson speculates that "there is often more to censorship than meets the eye," and that the earl, a supporter of George III, was having his revenge on Wilkes by reading the parody, because Wilkes was prosecuted for printing "a most scandalous, obscene and impious libel." Wilkes left for Paris under threat of arrest. He returned four years later and was jailed for twenty-two months, which only added to his reputation as a radical and a folk hero.

While he was still in prison, the voters of Middlesex elected Wilkes to Parliament no less than four times. Each time he was elected, the House of Commons (controlled by the king's party) refused to seat him, nominally because of his dirty-word behavior, but actually because of his championship of the American colonies. After the fourth election, the House of Commons dropped all pretense and simply ignored the election results, seating the government-supported candidate instead of Wilkes.

"Wilkes and Liberty" became a rallying cry throughout England and the American colonies, and many demonstrations were held in support of his cause. The issue, in the eyes of the angry populaces on both sides of the Atlantic, was the tyrannical manipulation of parliamentary privilege and the restraint of the people's right to elect their own representatives.

Thanks to the heroics of Wilkes and our founding fathers (I mean, founding parents), Americans live under the aegis of the First Amendment, which once protected a citizen's right to use language that is considered by others to be profane, tasteless, offensive, or vulgar. Modern protections offered by the First Amendment are becoming progressively more obscure, especially if one tries to formulate a workable rule from the case law that can be explained by someone who charges less than $150 an hour. The paltry sum you shelled out for this succinct, well-wrought volume is a widow's mite (I mean, a surviving spouse's mite) by comparison, probably half of what you pay for your annual income tax guide; and, at tax time, even the most virtuous citizen needs legal advice about swearing, because the government is not only telling you what to say, but what to pay, as well.

Does She or Doesn't She?

*Women who insist upon having the same options as
men would do well to consider the option of being the
strong, silent type.*

—Fran Lebowitz, as quoted by Jon Winokur in

The Portable Curmudgeon

*L*est the reader be emboldened by all this First Amendment froth and swagger off to work tomorrow, hoping to
regale the lunch table with his own version of 2 Live Crew's
"Me So Horny," I should warn him that the First Amendment does not apply in the workplace or in the classroom.
It was quietly amended in 1986, when the U.S. Supreme
Court issued its landmark opinion in *Meritor* v. *Vinson,* the
Court's first and most important case of sexual harassment
under Title VII, the federal statute banning discrimination
in employment.

Almost everyone—including almost all sensible men—

applauded the long-overdue *Meritor* opinion, because it formally outlawed sexual harassment of the quid pro quo (this for that) variety, making it illegal for a supervisor (usually a male) to implicitly or explicitly demand sexual favors from an employee (usually a female) in exchange for continued employment, promotions, raises, better grades, or better job evaluations.

But the *Meritor* opinion also created another cause of action, the "hostile environment" claim, when the Court quoted approvingly from the Equal Employment Opportunity Commission's guidelines defining "sexual harassment" under Title VII as

> **verbal or physical conduct of a sexual nature [having] the purpose or effect of unreasonably interfering with an individual's work performance or creating an intimidating, hostile, or offensive work environment.**

Expanding on this general language, the Court added that Title VII and the EEOC's guidelines afforded employees "the right to work in an environment free from discriminatory intimidation, ridicule, and insult."

Never mind that at least half the population (without regard to race, color, religion, sex, or national origin) suffers daily from what, in its considered opinion, is "intimidation, ridicule, and insult" in the workplace. And never mind that —as we saw in the last chapter—the First Amendment protects speech, even ridiculous and insulting speech, even profane and offensive speech. Despite all of that, most lower federal courts consider the EEOC's reference to "verbal conduct" as a ban on certain kinds of "verbal expression," or in the words of a federal district court in the Eastern District of Michigan:

> "verbal conduct of a sexual nature" . . . seems to be directed toward profane words and pictures that deal with sex.

In other words, it is directed at speech that the Supreme Court has already held in other contexts to be speech protected by the First Amendment.

Nine years after *Meritor,* this "hostile environment" theory hampers the free expression of a lot more than profane words and sexy pictures. Forget about swearing or expressing your opinions in the workplace. If you think I'm nitpicking, consider the following:

Professor Donald J. Silva was teaching a class on technical writing at the University of New Hampshire. Endeavoring to furnish the class with an example of a simile, he quoted a famous belly dancer named Little Egypt and said, "Belly dancing is like Jell-O on a plate with a vibrator under the plate."

Seven . . . ah, shall we say . . . women in the class filed formal complaints. A student-led tribunal found Professor Silva guilty of "verbal sexual harassment" and ordered him to apologize and undergo counseling. Silva sued and was suspended from his job. A federal district court recently held that the university had violated Silva's First Amendment right in punishing him. Message: If you have an extra twenty thousand dollars for attorney's fees and can afford to be suspended from your job for a year or so, you will probably be protected by the First Amendment and you may legally mention belly dancing. Otherwise, don't say the words "belly" and "dancing" in the same sentence.

Welcome to the brave new world of "verbal sexual harassment," better known as a "hostile" or "abusive environment" claim under the sprawling reach of Title VII. What is it? As Silva and others have discovered after being sued, fired, or both, it's whatever a woman or group of women find offensive on any given day. Nor is Silva's case an isolated incident, as the following cases show:

A federal district court judge in New York has held that use of gender-based terms such as "foreman" or "draftsman" could be harassment. The Second Circuit Court of Appeals affirmed this finding without opinion.

A federal court of appeals judge in an important sexual harassment case in the Sixth Circuit wrote in his dissenting opinion that a supervisor's desk plaque declaring "Even male chauvinist pigs need love"—together with what the judge considered "misogynous language" and pinups—was evidence of a violation of Title VII.

Remember, these are not standard "discrimination" cases, where someone gets fired, is paid less than someone else, is demoted or not hired because of their sex. These are not quid pro quo harassment cases, or cases where the plaintiffs were fondled or touched. These are federal lawsuits in which the plaintiffs are complaining that the workplace was too "hostile" or "abusive." Courts once required that the plaintiff at least suffer some kind of "injury," but that attempt at limiting the sweeping reach of the statute was snuffed out in 1993, when the Supreme Court rendered its second sexual harassment opinion.

In *Harris* v. *Forklift Systems,* the plaintiff sued her boss for saying things such as "You're a woman, what do you know" and "We need a man as a rental manager." Of course the pig said he was only joking and no harm was done, but joking is no longer permitted and harm need not be done. The Supreme Court stated emphatically that Title VII does not require that harassment must "seriously affect [an employee's] psychological well-being" or lead the plaintiff to "suffer injury." Harassment may be actionable if it simply alters the conditions of the victim's employment and creates an "abusive environment."

Hearing the hinges of the floodgates groaning with new harassment cases, Justice Antonin Scalia pointed out the obvious, that as long as Congress passes well-meaning statutes with "inherently vague statutory language," there's nothing to be done but give everyone the right to sue and let juries decide who should get damages. Writing in *Harris,* Scalia said:

> As a practical matter, today's holding lets virtually unguided juries decide whether sex-related conduct engaged in (or permitted by) an employer is egregious enough to warrant an award

> of damages. One might say that what constitutes
> "negligence" (a traditional jury question) is not
> much more clear and certain than what consti-
> tutes "abusiveness." Perhaps so. But the class
> of plaintiffs seeking to recover for negligence is
> limited to those who have suffered harm.

No such limitation encumbers the righteous indignation of harassment plaintiffs. In a Seventh Circuit Court of Appeals case, the sexual harassment plaintiff complained of "leers." In a federal district court in Kansas, a Title VII plaintiff sued her employer, alleging, among other things, that the company president made "goo goo eyes" at her.

The district court in the renowned case of *Robinson* v. *Jacksonville Shipyards* found an employer liable for sexual harassment based solely on "the presence in the workplace of pictures of women in various stages of undress and in sexually suggestive or submissive poses" and "sexually demeaning remarks and jokes." The pinup pictures were *Playboy* centerfolds and tool company calendars. The plaintiff specifically did *not* complain of any physical assaults or sexual propositions. Some pinups were posted in public view, but the court listed other sexually harassing behaviors, such as male employees reading offensive magazines in the workplace, or even carrying them in their back pockets.

The federal judge issued an order purging all "sexually suggestive" images (a category defined in sweeping terms) from the Jacksonville Shipyards. Not only were the employees enjoined from posting such images, they were barred from possessing, viewing, or displaying such materials in their own private workspaces at any time. The order also prohibited jokes and inappropriate comments "in the presence" of any employee who objects.

The operative term "sexually suggestive" was defined in the court's order:

> A picture will be presumed to be sexually suggestive if it depicts a person of either sex who is not fully clothed or in clothes that are not suited to or ordinarily accepted for the accomplishment of routine work in and around the shipyard and who is posed for the obvious purpose of displaying or drawing attention to private portions of his or her body.

True story! And from a federal district court judge, not some backwater state court judge. As the American Civil Liberties Union pointed out in its amicus curiae brief, this would effectively ban everything from family photos to reproductions of Michelangelo's *David* to *People* magazines from the workplace.

But even the *Jacksonville Shipyards* case pales when compared to a series of cases filed in the Minnesota state courts by female employees of Stroh's Brewery in St. Paul. Their complaint? Television ads for Old Milwaukee beer (produced by Stroh's Brewery) contribute to sexual harassment at the Stroh's plant, therefore the ads should be banned!

Sports fans and couch potatoes will recall the spots,

which featured a bunch of lugs on a fishing trip indulging in a fantasy of having the Swedish bikini team deliver them frosty mugs of Old Milwaukee. What's next? Litigation enjoining the employment of attractive female newscasters and sports announcers because it invites men to imagine them as subordinate sex objects?

Back to the real world, where restrictions on "harassing" behavior are not confined only to supervisors. Even a note from a pitiful, lovesick coworker is "abusive" and may constitute sexual harassment and a federal case of sex discrimination. In *Ellison* v. *Brady,* the alleged harasser was an agent of the Internal Revenue Service named Gray. He asked the plaintiff—his coworker, a woman agent—out for a drink after work. She declined, but suggested that they go out for lunch the following week. Gray waited a week and asked the plaintiff out to lunch, but she declined. A week later, Gray gave the plaintiff a note:

> I cried over you last night and I'm totally drained today. I have never been in such constant term oil [*sic*]. Thank you for talking with me. I could not stand to feel your hatred another day.

The plaintiff left the room and told a male coworker to advise Gray that she was not interested. Later, Gray sent the plaintiff another letter, telling her, among other things, "I have enjoyed you so much over these past few months. . . . I am obligated to you so much that if you want me to leave you alone I will. . . . If you want me to forget you entirely, I can not [*sic*] do that."

The plaintiff sued for sexual harassment. The district court concluded that the incident was "isolated and genuinely trivial." The plaintiff then appealed to the Ninth Circuit Court of Appeals, which reversed and held that "Gray's conduct was sufficiently severe and pervasive to alter the conditions of [plaintiff's] employment and create an abusive working environment."

In *Scott* v. *Sears, Roebuck & Co.*, the plaintiff complained that she had been "propositioned." When asked about her charge in a deposition, it turned out that the alleged harasser had asked her out to a restaurant for drinks after work.

That the correct finding of no liability is often eventually rendered in the federal appellate courts provides little solace to the hapless defendants and their companies, who spend years and fortunes litigating in the district court before obtaining a judgment on appeal. Instead of a litany of the awful abuses of gender-based harassment in the workplace, we should publish a few accounts of what it's like to endure three years of depositions, interrogatories, discipline at work, crucifixion in the media, and fear of losing your job —all because you were swinish enough to ask a woman for a date.

Dare we ask how many happily married, faithful husbands there are in the audience who had to ask their wives out more than once before they actually got a date with them? Those days are gone. Just as the common law developed a one-bite rule for owners of vicious dogs, men will henceforth be allowed one unwanted "advance," after which, if they guess wrong about whether their overtures are "wanted" or "unwanted," they will spend several years embroiled in federal litigation. No means no, even if you're offering to bring her a drink from the watercooler.

What if a male employee recites Andrew Marvell's "To His Coy Mistress in the Garden" at work: Is that sexual harassment? What if Groucho Marx were still around, took a job down at the plant, punched in, and said, "Women should be obscene and not heard"?

If the jury happened to consist of the sort of harridans who sued Donald Silva for saying "belly dancer," Groucho and his employer would get slapped with punitive damages. An application to the federal court of appeals or the Supreme Court would probably result in a verdict of "Not funny. Pay the money."

Concentration camp survivors may have to shut their blinds and let the Nazis march down their street in Skokie, Illinois, but women at work are entitled to an environment purged of any unpleasantness. In the words of Claudia Withers, the director of employment programs at the Women's Legal Defense Fund, "When women perceive that things like 'honey' and 'sweetie' make them uncomfortable on the job, it's against the law."

If constitutional scholars consider the FCC's victory over George Carlin and his seven dirty words as "singularly bad news," what are the First Amendment implications of a runaway "hostile environment" theory? The Supreme

Court has yet to grant certiorari in a case where the First Amendment has been raised as an affirmative defense, but commentators including prominent feminists of various ideological persuasions are writing about, and litigating, the issues.

The most thorough catalogue of cases in which verbal expression formed all or part of a finding of liability under Title VII may be found in Kingsley R. Browne's "Title VII as Censorship: Hostile-Environment Harassment and the First Amendment" (*Ohio State Law Journal* 52, 1991, p. 481) and in Eugene Volokh's "Freedom of Speech and Workplace Harassment" (*UCLA Law Review* 13, 1992, p. 1791). Professor Browne poses the following provocative hypothetical:

> Suppose, for example, an employer had a policy of imposing discipline against any employee who used profanity in front of a woman. The assumption that women as a group may be more offended by profanity than men as a group seems like just the sort of stereotype that Title VII was intended to erase. Just as it may be empirically true that women as a group are more offended by profanity than men, it also may be empirically true that women as a group are more nurturant than men, but courts have interpreted Title VII to prohibit reliance on the latter generalization, and it is unclear why the

two generalizations should enjoy different status.

It is precisely this dilemma that has created the booming
market for highly paid "consultants" and gender-equity
specialists that sprang up in the wake of the Anita Hill–
Clarence Thomas hearings. This army of employment discrimination lawyers, psychologists, sociologists, and anyone
else who could quickly put together a résumé with the
words "sexual harassment" on it tours the nation's busi-
nesses conducting seminars designed to explain the concept
of a hostile environment in the context of laws against
sexual harassment.

The work is quite lucrative because it's impossible to
explain the theory in less than a full day's worth of billable
hours. To understand it, factory workers, construction
workers, and dockhands must have the mental agility neces-
sary for what F. Scott Fitzgerald called "negative capability,"
or the ability "to hold two opposed ideas in the mind at the
same time."

It goes something like this: Women as a group are equal,
as intelligent and capable as men. Gender should play no
role in any employment decision. Any suggestion that
women should be treated differently because of their gender
is anathema. As one district court explained it, Title VII
"rejects the notion of 'romantic paternalism' towards
women." Don't hold the door open for them or call them
dearie or sweetie, they are full and equal partners. However,

it is also extremely important that you don't use profanity or refer to sex in any way, shape, or form around female employees, because they need special protection from abusiveness, ridicule, and insults at work—because of their gender. Understand?

The paradox, along with the even more volatile issue of pornography, has created a yawning chasm in the feminist movement. On one side are the run-with-the-wolves feminists, such as Nadine Strossen (president of the American Civil Liberties Union), author of *Defending Pornography: Free Speech, Sex, and the Fight for Women's Rights* and of law-review articles on the same subject, in which she has stated:

> "Protectionist" measures designed to shelter women from sexually explicit expression in the workplace conform to the general pattern of gender-specific "protectionist" measures, by actually operating to women's detriment. Regardless of the benevolent intent of such measures, they in fact reflect and reinforce a patronizing, paternalistic view of women's sexuality that is inconsistent with women's full equality. This point has been made in a context highly analogous to the present one: The controversy over whether certain "pornography," defined as "subordinating" to women, should be censored. While some feminists advocate such censorship, others oppose it, in part because of its paternal-

istic effect. ["Sexual Harassment in the Workplace: Accommodating Free Speech and Gender
Equality Values," in *Free Speech Yearbook 1993*]

On the other side of the question are the Carrie Nation
zealots who belong to the antipornography wing of the
feminist movement headed up by Catherine MacKinnon
and Andrea Dworkin. These are the so-called victim feminists—activists who have been working for decades to pass
antipornography statutes. They adhere to the notion that
women are delicate flowers in need of laws to protect them
from "graphic, sexually explicit materials that subordinate
women through pictures and words." Men presumably require no such protection because they are hearty and, well,
manly creatures; it takes more than a word or a picture to
subordinate a man, a woman is a different matter.

As Strossen points out, these attempts at protective legislation sound a lot like statutes from the last century that
continually lumped women with children and the mentally
infirm—innocents requiring assistance and protection
from the depredations of men and commerce. As late as
1971, in the First Amendment case *Cohen* v. *California,*
discussed earlier, the Supreme Court thought it important
to note in its opinion that when Paul Cohen wore his "FUCK
THE DRAFT" jacket into the courthouse, "There were
women and children present in the corridor."

In the end, it all comes back to the kind of question the
judge asked Shannon Faulkner's lawyers when they came
back to court complaining that the Citadel was going to

shave her head before allowing her to enroll at the all-male military school: Just how equal do you want her to be treated?

As Robert Wright, author of *The Moral Animal,* put it recently in *The New Republic:*

> The more protection you want to provide women, the harder it is to argue that they don't by their nature need special protection; the more often you see them victimized, the stronger the implication that they are by nature victims, weaker than men. That is why some feminists resist MacKinnon's broader definitions of sexual harassment and of rape, and her view of pornography as an assault on women. [November 28, 1994]

Asking men and women to work together without referring to sex is like asking for a production of *Hamlet* without the ghost. Kingsley Browne separates messages suppressed by sexual harassment litigation into two messages, both of which would be protected speech anywhere else, perhaps even in the workplace: the first, a "hostility message" that women "do not belong in the workplace"; the second, a "sexuality message . . . that the harasser views the plaintiff in particular or women in general in a sexual light." The latter message is the one that most irks the victim feminists. But why? As Browne observes:

> [T]here is no necessary contradiction in viewing
> one's colleague (or even one's subordinate) si-
> multaneously as an attractive sexual being and
> a competent co-worker. Indeed, the societal
> ideal for marriage is that the parties to the mar-
> riage view each other as intellectual equals, as
> autonomous persons, *and* as desirable romantic
> partners. Acceptance of the suggestion that a
> relationship can be based on either mutual re-
> spect or lust, but not both, would not bode well
> for the future of marriage in our society.

The current mania for "hostile environment" sexual harassment claims is simply an inverted demand for politeness, the same Victorian strictures from the nineteenth
century that required gentlemen to behave themselves when
they were around the fair sex: don't spit in the parlor, don't
curse, don't scratch yourself. The proper posture for a male
who makes a woman feel uncomfortable is a blanket, abject
apology, the sort of sweeping *apologia pro vita sua* offered
most recently by Washington's governor, Mike Lowry. Fac-
ing a complaint by his former deputy press secretary that
he sexually harassed her, Lowry offered this apology for
behavior he did not describe: "I have learned that some
people are uncomfortable, and whoever that might be—
anybody I've ever made feel uncomfortable—I apologize to.
But I have never, ever done anything that was ever meant
to make anybody feel uncomfortable."

God help him if he had! Can you imagine a man who would dare to express an opinion or make a stray remark, knowing full well that there is every chance in the world that someone, somewhere, will experience fleeting discomfort as a direct result of his thoughtless behavior?

Women are fragile waifs who shouldn't be subjected to swearing, dirty jokes, and frank sexual remarks. Either this is true and women *are* different, as well as unable to compete in a rough-and-tumble workplace without special protections, or it is false and we have no need for laws prohibiting verbal sexual harassment.

So the First Amendment should now be read as follows: "The government shall make no law abridging the freedom of speech, except to protect women from ridicule and insult in the workplace." Forget about the f-word at work. In fact, forget about expressing your opinions on the subject of anything having to do with race or gender or ethnicity, unless those opinions comport with the opinions of the Equal Employment Opportunity Commission.

I am not arguing that the First Amendment protects someone from being fired for saying ridiculous and insulting things. The Constitution protects citizens from big government, not from the depredations of private employers—statutes, such as Title VII, are designed to do that, but statutes must be constitutional. In other words, the government may not directly silence offensive speech, nor may it get around the Constitution by passing a law requiring employers to silence speech. Nothing in the Constitution prevents an employer from spontaneously making rules requiring civility or politeness in the workplace, nor does it restrain an employer's right to fire people for being uncivil. The constitutional problem occurs when a *government* passes a law such as Title VII (which is now being interpreted as a ban on certain kinds of speech) or when an employer bans certain kinds of speech for fear of being sued under vaguely worded government statutes.

Imagine the implications of the government passing a law banning the discussion of political issues in the workplace. Do we really want to make it a federal crime to say, "Women are weak" or "Men are pigs"? Because that is where the sweeping efforts of employers to comply with the EEOC's regulations are headed. Currently eight male employees of the female-dominated company Jenny Craig are suing their bosses for sex discrimination. These men are complaining about an overabundance of girl talk in the workplace, and because their bosses said abusive things to them, such as "You're pretty sensitive for a guy." Perhaps nothing surprises the fawning, dutifully sensitive male of the nineties more than the perfect equanimity of certain feminists who complain about being stereotyped and discriminated against in one breath, and in the next dismiss half the human race as male pigs and sexists. These "differences" used to make the world go 'round. Now they are the stuff of six-week jury trials and massive damage awards.

No fair-minded male begrudges the bouquet of rights handed out by Title VII to disadvantaged minorities and to women (who constitute a majority of the population), as long as those rights are confined predominantly to equal pay for equal work, equal job opportunities, and termination without regard to race, creed, color, sex, and so on. But a lopsided entitlement to be free of the unpleasantness of human interaction?

One pernicious notion that surfaces every time a legislature creates a new protected group is that the explosion of antidiscrimination legislation merely provides gays or disabled citizens or fat people the same rights enjoyed by the rest of us. That fallacy is easily dispelled by the following hypothetical.

Evil Earl, a white male employer, strolls out onto the factory floor one morning and fires five people. Earl tells the first one: "You are *the* dumbest person I have ever met. On top of that, you're a jerk. Go find a job somewhere else."

Earl tells employee number two: "I detest red ties. You are wearing a red tie. Get lost."

Employee number three is a male with a lisp and effeminate mannerisms. Earl says: "I don't know for sure, but I think you may be a homosexual and I don't want any fucking faggots working here. Watch your step on the way out, nancy boy."

Employee number four is told: "You are the ugliest person I have ever seen. Do you expect me to inflict a sight like that on my customers and employees five days a week? Go get a job in a circus."

Candidate five is a woman. Earl says, "We don't want any bitches working here. Go away."

Question: How many of the five employees—all of whom have been unfairly, even maliciously treated—have a cause of action for employment discrimination under federal law, which bans employment discrimination on the basis of age under the Age Discrimination in Employment Act, on the basis of disability under the Americans with Disabilities Act, and on the basis of "race, color, religion, sex, or national origin" under Title VII? Only the woman can state a claim under Title VII. The rest of us can be fired for any reason, or for no reason, under the employment-at-will doctrine, which is still the law in the majority of states.

The liberal response would be to draft amendments to Title VII or some other federal statute, adding more protected groups and banning discrimination on the basis of jerkiness, stupidity, red ties, homosexuality, overweightedness, and ugliness. But each time a new protected group is added, 20,000 new complaints of discrimination and 40,000 new lawyers appear, and federal courtrooms become massive human resources departments. Big-time federal litigation, employing judges, juries, clerks, paralegals, lawyers —generating huge legal bills and reams of paper—all amass to settle a single question of paramount social importance: Was Ruby McDuff fired from XYZ Corporation because she is stupid and lazy, or because she is sixty-two years old and a woman? Or maybe it was because she likes to nap at work? But what if her napping is caused by a disability— narcolepsy, for instance? Then she can't be fired without her employer first making reasonable accommodations for her, like getting Ruby a couch and an alarm clock. Maybe she's just lazy, but before too long it will be illegal to discriminate against people because they are lazy. What if she has a biologically determined low metabolism and can't help it? Is that fair? Soon Congress will pass a law making it illegal for an employer to consider intelligence a job qualification, because it discriminates against stupid people.

These rights take on a life of their own and swell to Gargantuan proportions. When the initial version of Title VII came to the floor of Congress in 1964, it outlawed discrimination on the basis of race, creed, religion, and national origin. Sex was added minutes before the legislation passed, with no contemplation on the part of Congress that the term would one day forbid everything from pregnancy discrimination to saying "honey" in the workplace.

The EEOC is currently sitting on approximately 97,000 unresolved claims of discrimination, together with an estimated 100,000 new claims filed in 1994 alone. Eighty-five percent of these claims are ultimately rejected for lack of evidence or are withdrawn by the employee. About 12 percent are resolved in the worker's favor without a formal finding of discrimination. This leaves approximately 3 percent of all complaints showing enough solid evidence of discrimination or harassment to warrant litigation, and we've seen some of the examples of what "solid" evidence looks like.

Men have no right to work in an environment free of harassment, ridicule, and insult, and don't they know it. The next time you are subjected to ridicule and insult in the break rooms and locker rooms at work, just try claiming you are entitled to work in an environment free of ridicule and insult, and see what happens. Several members of the allegedly stronger sex already tried it and lost. These cases show that the unspoken prerequisite in the majority of Title VII hostile environment claims is *not* that you suffer harassment because of your sex, but that you suffer harassment because of your sex *and* that the message conveyed is antifeminist or antifemale.

In *Goluszek* v. *Smith,* an Illinois district court case, a guy sued his employer because he believed that his male coworkers' foul language created a sexually hostile work environment. Don't laugh, it's not funny. It's a cruel world out there. Anthony Goluszek was a shy, unsophisticated fellow who was exquisitely sensitive to comments about sex. Male coworkers showed him pictures of naked women, told him they would get him "fucked," and poked him in the ass with a stick, all conduct that would get the defendants beheaded in any federal district, if they had done it to a woman.

The federal district court agreed that Goluszek was harassed because of his sex—male—but it held that the harassment stated no claim under Title VII. Unlike Goluszek's case, said the court, in a valid Title VII harassment case, "the offender is saying by words or actions that the victim is inferior because of the victim's sex." The court reasoned that the harassment Goluszek suffered could not have conveyed the message that he was inferior because of his sex, because he was a male in a male-dominated environment.

See the beauty of it? The hostile-environment components of Title VII protect everyone—male and female—from harassment based on sex. But you must be a woman to state a claim if the environment is male-dominated.

The essential antifemale component can be further highlighted with another hypothetical.

In 1991 they tried to keep a guy off the Supreme Court because of things he *said,* as in because he engaged in speech normally protected by the First Amendment. Let's pretend he actually said everything he was accused of saying. Nobody ever accused him of touching anybody, or of "propositioning" anybody. He was accused of being a male on the make, a single guy making a suggestive comment to a single woman who went to lunch with him. He was accused of floating one out there to see if there were any nibbles. (None of us have ever done anything like that, but we've seen others do it, and it's fairly common behavior for a young, unattached, disgusting beast looking for romance.)

Pretending again that he actually said those unspeakable things, let's also pretend that instead of Anita Hill, a guy came forward, Adam Hill, a man. Adam is a Yale lawyer who worked at the EEOC with Clarence Thomas. And Adam says, "I don't think Clarence Thomas should sit on the Supreme Court because one time I heard him say there was a pubic hair in his Coke, and another time I heard him say he liked to watch porno movies."

The Senate Judiciary Committee would have stifled a yawn and said, "Just how many frequent flier miles did you rack up coming here to tell us *that*?"

Do you get it yet? The Fifth Circuit has stated twice that

"harassment by a male supervisor against a male subordinate does not state a claim under Title VII even though the harassment has sexual overtones." As of this writing, the federal circuits are split on the issues of same-sex sexual harassment, with the majority of federal courts declaring that there is no cause of action for male-on-male sexual harassment. That there should even be a question shows the essentially feminist underpinnings of Title VII as interpreted by the courts.

Feminists love to catalogue the lurid details of abusive sexual harassment, a tactic designed to convince the rest of us that only pervasive and intrusive government regulation and civil litigation can protect the victims. As any male steelworker will tell you, the details of male-on-male "harassment" are much worse, it's just that men live with it every day, and usually respond in kind by saying, "Fuck off!" and then take their chances with the fallout. Feminists counter that women don't have that luxury because men are often bigger, stronger, and more threatening than their female victims, which makes you wonder what a guy is supposed to do when a male twice his size walks up to him on the job and says, "I've decided to make you my bitch."

If it's size and strength the victims need protection from, then the laws should ban discrimination based upon size and strength, not gender.

In *Vandeventer* v. *Wabash National Corp.*, one of the plaintiffs, Douglas Feltner, was eliminated early from the case because he was a male and the other plaintiffs were females. Feltner complained to his employer that one of his coordinators, a crew or team leader, had aimed comments such as "drop down," "dick sucker," and "crawl under the table" at Feltner. The court also noted that the supervisor "made a comment wondering whether Mr. Feltner could perform fellatio without his false teeth," and "also asked Mr. Feltner if he would go with him to a gay bar."

Citing a string of federal cases, the district court dismissed Feltner's claim because "Title VII is aimed . . . at an atmosphere of oppression by a 'dominant' gender."

One can sympathize with the federal judiciary's attempt to put some kind of a lid on the class of eligible plaintiffs, because, along with drug cases, civil rights cases are engulfing federal courtrooms in a morass of litigation. Drugs and discrimination—the pet peeves of right Republicans and left Democrats respectively—are jamming federal courtrooms with the prosecution of substance abusers, discriminators, and harassers. Federal juries are empaneled for two-week trials, during which time they must listen attentively to one witness after another recount all the dirty jokes and racial or ethnic slurs they've heard in the workplace, and to four different accounts of whether the president of the company really made "goo goo eyes" at the plaintiff. Soon every citizen will be entitled under federal law to work only with coemployees who have good manners, healthy recreational habits, and inoffensive speech.

The ever-broadening view of "discrimination" is turning federal courtrooms into giant personnel departments for employee grievances, because, thanks to the popularity of "civil rights" and the largesse of state and federal legislatures, almost everyone is a member of a protected group, with one notable exception: white males under forty. Someone in Washington recently added up all the groups who qualify for special treatment under federal affirmative action programs and found the total to include somewhere between two-thirds and three-fourths of the population, prompting Senator Daniel Patrick Moynihan to observe, "That's a lot of minority." And this "minority" of the population is well educated when it comes to inventorying and husbanding (I mean, midwifing) their rights. Movies-of-the-week and relentlessly thorough seminars conducted by gender specialists have endowed even high school students with exquisitely sensitive radar capability when it comes to detecting anything that will allow them to state a claim for "harassment" and "equality rights."

But this unrestrained passion for equality, at a certain point, starts to resemble Communist ideology and Orwellian Newspeak, because the accompanying censorship of speech to eliminate even the whiff of inequality reminds one of Socialist Realism under Stalin, when the government decreed suitable topics for art, literature, and political discourse and banned all others. Kingsley Browne resurrected Alexis de Tocqueville's observation that

> democratic nations are at all times fond of equality, but there are certain epochs at which the passion they entertain for it swells to the height of fury.... Tell them not that, by this blind surrender of themselves to an exclusive

passion, they risk their dearest interests: they are deaf. Show them not freedom escaping from their grasp whilst they are looking another way: they are blind, or rather, they can discern but one object to be desired in the universe. . . .

I think that democratic communities have a natural taste for freedom: left to themselves, they will seek it, cherish it, and view any privation of it with regret. But for equality, their passion is ardent, insatiable, incessant, invincible: they call for equality in freedom: and if they cannot obtain that, they still call for equality in slavery.

Censorship in the name of equality sounds suspiciously like one of those *Animal Farm* slogans—how about: "All Words Are Equal, Except Hostile and Abusive Words, Which Are Less Equal than Others." Just as *law* consists of the common law and so-called black letter law, municipal ordinances and the tax code, civil rights statutes, the U.S. Constitution, and the Treaty of Versailles, *language* includes spirit and letter, speech and the printed page, dialect and slang, not to mention the upper-class status and graduate degree of a formal dictionary definition. Making the public utterance of certain words—what the EEOC and some federal judges call "verbal conduct"—a crime is one censorious stratagem. Another is to deprive certain words of their right to equal coverage in our nation's dictionaries. The first requires the political power of those who don't want to hear certain words, the second requires prudery and an unprofessional bias on the part of those who make and publish dictionaries.

Psychiatrists and linguists know that there are no intrinsically bad words, just as musicians know that there are no intrinsically bad notes. The same words we use to ridicule, insult, offend, and produce what the EEOC and the courts call "verbal conduct of a sexual nature" can also be used to create novels, poems, songs, prayers, and, perhaps most important, jokes (every one a "tiny revolution," according to George Orwell).

As we have discussed, the best way to appreciate the ambivalence of "bad," "dirty," or "hateful" words is to examine a few whose negative charge is waning but still in recent memory. Like those ambiguous perceptual figures in psychology books, a shift in perspective can turn formerly prohibited words like *hell* or *shit* into education and entertainment, excursions into the human psyche.

The Bad Place

Hell *fills so large a part of the American vocabulary,
that it will probably be worn out in a few years more.*
—L. H. MERRYWEATHER, AMERICAN SPEECH, 1931

*Then she told me all about the bad place, and I said I
wished I was there. She got mad, then, but I didn't
mean no harm. All I wanted was to go somewheres; all
I wanted was a change, I warn't particular. She said it
was wicked to say what I said; said she wouldn't say it
for the whole world; she was going to live so as to go to
the good place. Well, I couldn't see no advantage in
going where she was going, so I made up my mind I
wouldn't try for it.*
—MARK TWAIN, THE ADVENTURES OF HUCKLEBERRY FINN

*T*hese days the Widow Douglas and Miss Watson are gender-equity specialists, calling us down to the Human Resources Department to fill out an incident report on our
use of biased language. We are given unshirted hell for

saying "mankind" and "honey" and threatened with the secular-humanist equivalent of damnation: the witness stand as a defendant in sexual harassment litigation. We do penance, squirm in our chairs and watch the Gender Awareness Video Workshop, all the while wishing we were out on a raft in the middle of the Mississippi, where we could unbutton and smoke a pipe, speak freely, and crack a few dirty jokes.

It's virtuous people who give Heaven a bad name, especially when they attempt to impose their moral rectitude on the rest of us under penalty of law. One gander at Sensitivity Heaven and an earful of correct language from the equality police are enough to inspire an abiding affection for Hell and its occupants.

Hell is probably the most acceptable swearword, tolerated even in polite conversation, especially in the South and Midwest. It is useful in establishing rapport with a new audience—a few ingenious employments of the word slipped into otherwise colorless conversation allows you to determine whether your listeners find swearing objectionable: if so, you might consider shifting to the more offensive words dealt with in previous chapters, or you can do the only proper thing and cuss blue thunderbolts until you singe their eyebrows. Either way, starting off with *hell* signals your own appreciation of colorful language and may encourage a like-minded devil (lurking somewhere at the fringes of the cocktail crowd) to spit on her or his hands and hoist the black flag.

Using *hell* or *damn* puts you in the company of the Devil

and Mark Twain, who said, "Let us swear while we may, for in heaven it will not be allowed." And Heaven is not far off, if federal officials from the Department of Hate Speech have anything to say about it. You may think of *hell* and *the devil* as garlic in the stew of good conversation, but there are hall monitors waiting for you on our nation's campuses who want to drive you, with whips of steel, into speech paradise —a place where no one speaks ill of anyone else and there is no name-calling. These politically correct types are *all hell on* politeness or *all hell for* diversity. If you don't say things in a certain precise way, they will give you *hell with the hide off,* until you adopt their terminology, which is all *hell-bent and crooked.*

A person who freely salts her or his lines with *hell* is probably, at least subconsciously, obsessed with eschatology, or the study of the final things. What is the ultimate destiny or purpose of mankind and the world? Why was the universe created and what is our ultimate place in it? I'll be go to helled if I know, and damn your ugly eyes for asking, I was just trying to explain what eschatology means.

Unlike the other offensive words featured in this book, *hell* is first and foremost a place, instead of an activity (*fuck*), a substance (*shit*), a bodily process (*fuck* and *shit*) a body part, a slur, a stereotype, or an epithet. Despite the attempts of some modern theologians to describe Hell as the "pain of loss" or "the remorse of conscience," such a concept was entirely too theoretical for the ancients. For them, Hell was real—a place of evil things and evil people.

The Bad Place

According to the Old Testament, certain idolaters worshipped the god Moloch and offered sacrifice to him by burning children alive in a valley south of Jerusalem called Gehenna; the place was known as Tophet (which in Hebrew means "a place to be spat upon"). King Josiah abolished these practices and ordered Tophet to be filled with corpses, ordure, and sacrilegious objects. A perpetual fire was kept burning to consume the dead bodies and filth and to render the place unfit for further worship of false gods. Over the years, Gehenna became a metaphor, after the fashion of East St. Louis, New Jersey, or certain portions of Washington, D.C.

Those who insist that Hell is a man-made invention take nothing away from the magnificence of the place, for, as Alice K. Turner pointed out in *The History of Hell:* "The landscape of Hell is the largest shared construction project in imaginative history, and its chief architects have been creative giants—Homer, Virgil, Plato, Augustine, Dante, Bosch, Michelangelo, Milton, Goethe, Blake, and more." We may be uncertain about whether such a fantastical place exists, but entire civilizations, ancient and modern, have lived in terror of it, sworn by it; endured lifetimes of self-sacrifice and died slow, painful deaths in the hope of avoiding it.

Sartre said, "Hell is other people"; Shelley said, "Hell is a city much like London." But the more interesting modern observations about Hell propose that it is a projection of ourselves, an extension or representation of what can happen in *this* life, and not just a faraway hereafter. In the foreword to Robert Pinsky's new verse translation, *The Inferno of Dante,* John Freccero explains:

> In Dante's poem, Hell is the parody of a city, point zero in the scale of cosmic love. Like Augustine's City of Man, it is meant to represent the social consequences of insatiable desire when it remains earthbound.... At the same time, it may also be thought of as a radical representation of the world in which we live, stripped of all temporizing and all hope.

Shakespeare captured the same idea with characteristic concision when he said, "Hell is empty, and all the devils are here!" As we saw earlier, an insatiable desire for equality becomes a religion with its own earthbound Hell, where individual expression and achievement, humor and freedom are all viewed with suspicion, because they may contribute to Unfairness. A belief in the equality of all can be a personal virtue, until the government imposes it by decree, in which case it becomes just another obligation to conform.

As the narrator in Dostoyevsky's *Notes from the Underground* observed, Man will swear out loud if only to prove that he is not a piano key, and as soon as everyone agrees that twice two is four, some provocateur will declare that twice two is five. When Heaven is required by subparts A through F of a federal statute, certain people will insist on the opposite if only out of spite, and evil words have always been at least as important as misdeeds in getting the job done. As John Ciardi, one of Dante's translators, observed, there's no telling from age to age what kind of hate speech qualifies someone for damnation:

> It has often seemed to me that the offensive language of Protestantism is obscenity; the offensive language of Catholicism is profanity or blasphemy: one offends on a scale of unmentionable words for bodily function, the other on a scale of disrespect for the sacred. Dante places the Blasphemous in Hell as the worst of the Violent against God and His Works, but he has no category for punishing those who use four-letter words. [*Inferno,* Mentor Classic Edition]

My feeling is, if we are going to have federal employment laws forbidding insult and ridicule in the workplace, these statutes should be construed to include the ultimate in abusiveness, namely, oaths and curses that explicitly attempt to inflict eternal harassment in the form of damnation of one's immortal soul to Hell.

Think about it! Which is worse? Saying, "You're a woman, what do you know?" or "Goddamn your Christian soul to Hell for all eternity!"

Lucky for us, the vague wording of these laws never changes, so an amendment is never needed. The only requirement is for the courts to conclude—as God knows they should!—that statements alluding to or threatening another person with eternal damnation (including but not limited to "Devil take you," "To Hell with you," "Go to Hell," or "Goddamn you") are by their very nature abusive, because they alter the conditions of the victim's employment, creating a hostile environment. Triple punitive damages could be imposed for especially offensive references to the underworld or its inhabitants, such as:

1. Go to Hell and pump thunder;
2. Go to Hell and eat rats with the Devil's pitchfork;
3. Hell's bells and pork pies!;
4. Hell's bells and buckets of blood!;
5. Epithets such as "imp of Satan," "jackdaw of Belial," or "Beelzebub's henchman."

Amending Title VII is unnecessary for another good reason: the statute already bans discrimination on the basis of "race, color, religion, sex, or national origin." It's plain on the face of the law that "religion" would include the right of any individual to worship or associate with any deity or supernatural being of her or his choosing, including Satan. Therefore, calling someone a *devil,* a *hellpuke,* a *hellion,* a *hellhound,* a *hellcat,* or a *hellpup* would constitute abusiveness and harassment based solely on the victim's religious affiliations. A thoughtless remark such as "idle hands are the Devil's workshop" assumes that ethically different people with alternative religious beliefs are lazy. This is the kind of blatantly discriminatory remark that causes real pain to the morally challenged individual, whose hurt feelings can only be remedied by a sizable punitive damage award.

The male pig obnoxious enough to say something like "At certain times of the month, Wilma is the Devil's own hellion," or, "The serving wench who carried me home from the tavern had one hell-busting rack of hooters on her," could be sued for sex discrimination *and* for religious discrimination, which would make for twice as much justice in the workplace.

Feminists complain about the maleness of God and the femaleness of Eve, but so far no one has complained about Satan's masculinity. ("That's easily explained," opine the man-haters, "men are evil.") The Devil has been called a gentleman who never goes where he is not welcome, the prince of darkness and a gentleman, a liar and the father of it, one who can cite Scripture for his purpose, one who prays only when he's out to deceive you, and one who speaks the truth on occasion. He's been called God's ape, an egotist, one of the principal objects of American reverence, and a god who has been bounced for conduct unbecoming a gentleman. But his name is invoked infrequently these days. People nowadays show more respect for the Devil as a person having an alternative ethical system, someone with his own special abilities and problems in the universe, and they are less likely to stereotype him or pass judgment on him before they walk a few hundred miles in his shoes.

What's needed is a politically correct, inoffensive moniker for the Devil, something like the Prince of Darkness (whoops, that's sexist). How about the Royal Family Member of Darkness (elitist and classist)? How about the Family Member of Darkness (discriminates against homosexuals and childless couples and makes antiquated, biased assumptions about communal living arrangements)? How about the Person of Darkness (racist because it assumes that those associated with darker colors are somehow evil)? How about Person of Badness, or simply Evil Being (assumes that some people are inherently "better" than others)?

Why not use the favored tactic of making a virtue out of the victim's special needs? How about the Spiritual Being Who Would Rather Rule in Hell than Serve in Heaven? At any rate, there is a modern aversion to taking Satan's name in vain; instead, most simply worship the Devil in their own quiet ways without seeking recognition for their misbehavior.

You may thoughtlessly and insensitively assume that Heaven is a "good" and "desirable" place and that Hell is "bad" and "undesirable," but not everyone shares your bigoted and chauvinistic ethical assumptions. Fortunately, federal laws against bias also forbid "place" discrimination, as a result of 1989 amendments that broadened the Fair Housing Act of 1968.

According to an article in *The Wall Street Journal* (November 3, 1994), the Pennsylvania Association of Realtors, the Pennsylvania Newspaper Association, and the Pennsylvania Human Relations Commission recently issued guidelines against the use of certain words in real-estate ads, including: "bachelor pad," "landmark," "couples," "newly-weds," "mature," "older seniors," "adults," "single," "children," "senior citizen," "setting up housekeeping," and "traditional neighborhood," to name but a few. In Pennsylvania, it's best not to describe the neighborhood at all, because the guidelines forbid using adjectives such as "exclusive," "private," "integrated," "established," or "close to" any local structure (probably because it discriminates against people who are not close to the same structure).

In 1994, the Fair Housing Council of Suburban Philadelphia filed lawsuits against landlords (and ladies) and three newspapers asking for more than $1 million in damages due to discriminatory ads. An ad describing a house in Chester as a "rare find" was pulled because the house was located in a black area, which suggested that it was "rare" for blacks to live in nice houses. Describing property as having an "ocean view" or being "within walking distance" of some local landmark discriminates against disabled persons (the blind and the crippled). If you say you have a "family room" you are discriminating against homosexuals and childless couples. A "master bedroom," a "mother-in-law suite," or a "bachelor pad" are all hopelessly sexist and forbidden.

The *Hunterdon County Democrat* in New Jersey will not accept ads using "professional," "nonsmoker," "quiet," or "exclusive." The words "ideal for" are also forbidden.

In Milwaukee, Beverly Schnell, a fifty-year-old divorced woman, spent three years in court fighting off a lawsuit brought by the Milwaukee Fair Housing Council because she had advertised a preference for a "mature Christian handyman" as a tenant to rent an apartment in her suburban home.

In Salem, Oregon, a newspaper was sued for religious discrimination because it ran an ad with a logo of the Easter Bunny and the invidiously discriminatory words "Happy Easter." Another complaint in Oregon sought damages for the phrase "convenient to jogging trails" because it discriminated against the disabled.

How about "Good house for sale"? Oh, I see, you want to discriminate against evil people?

Maybe it is possible to enforce equality of place by way of housing legislation. Or maybe under some future, high-minded regime, it will be unlawful to discriminate against "bad" places where "bad" things seem to happen because "bad" people live there. In the next century, perhaps our motives for relocating will be examined by government officials performing a housing audit and charged with determining whether in selecting our new home we have illegally discriminated against lower-class neighborhoods with bad schools and high crime rates in favor of upper-middle-class neighborhoods with good schools and low crime rates. Shouldn't that be against the law? What if someday studies show that we have this despicable need for hellish places because they enhance our appreciation of heavenly ones, the same way we need infernal imagery as a point of reference ("point zero") for ascending to the divine?

The Bad Place

Instead of a place where malefactors are consigned to do penance for their crimes, what if Hell is a refuge for misfits and misanthropes who shun the enforced good cheer and fellowship of the human race and are embarrassed at the prospect of meeting their Creator? What if, as so often seems the case, jailbirds fall in with those of similar plumage and prefer the camaraderie of the local tavern over the company of good citizens indulging civilized appetites in a place where you have to keep track of your salad forks and wine glasses? What if, like Huck, we simply cannot bear another exemplary display of virtue? More to the point, what if we all have a little bit of the Devil or She-Devil in us, and sometimes, when churchyards yawn under a full moon, we get the urge to go somewhere and network with the demon or demonette in everyone else and do some of that bitter business the day quakes to look on, or indulge in some sweet, forbidden frolic?

This yearning for separate quarters dovetails nicely with the cravings of the virtuous and the well mannered, who need a place to send hate speakers, word criminals, and other souls damned by the EEOC for "verbal or physical conduct of a sexual nature [having] the purpose or effect of unreasonably interfering with an individual's work performance or creating an intimidating, hostile, or offensive work environment." As we'll see later, it is uncertain whether Hell was invented to satisfy God's need for justice, Man's need for revenge, or the sinner's need for a place to get two shots of Wild Turkey and a beer chaser. In any event, it's never enough to herd the wicked off to a pit where they can discriminate against one another forever. We need to punish them for their hateful conduct, and then we need skyboxes and Court TV overlooking the coliseums of Hell, so we can enjoy the show from a safe distance.

In the arsenal of swearwords, *hell* is a shibboleth by which the fallen can recognize one another before they die or get sued. Vulgarians use it a lot because they are speaking fondly of their future home. They are subconsciously expressing longing and affection for a place where their cursing will be met with applause, instead of scolding and litigation; where their uncouth deportment will stand them in good graces, and their coarse language will be served up in testimonials around a roaring hearth; where they'll spend their days basking in fellowship and good cheer, warmed by toasts of "Short draughts and long swallows, men! It's the Devil's swill, Hell's own broth, and hotter than Satan's hoof!"

These louts are so fond of Hell they are constantly telling other people to go there, or imploring God to damn various individuals or objects to Hell forthwith. Damn this, goddamn that—it's plain that the hooligans are trying to fill Hell with everything they'll need upon arrival. And when a vulgarian says, "Go to Hell!" or, "Goddamn you!" one should accept the compliment gracefully, because it means this picturesque soul would like to spend the rest of eternity gambling and playing cards with you, trading insults and bawdy limericks, abusing you for a scoundrel and a fool, roasting tired jokes and chestnuts with you in the sulphur pits and crackling bonfires of Hades.

According to the doctrine of infralapsarianism, God foresaw and permitted the Fall of Man; if that's the case, Man needs somewhere to land. I know just the place. I woke up there the other night at two in the morning, the Devil's dinner hour. I lifted my head off the bar in a clip joint on the wrong side of Dogtown, Hell's half-acre tucked away in a basement under a storefront, crawling with tough customers in chains and Hell's Angels' T-shirts. Wilma was sitting next to me doing a devil's tattoo on the bar with a set of red-hot, sculpted fingernails. She had a wicked pair of legs in black fishnets wrapped around a bar stool, a black leather jacket, glossy as Satan's shoeshine, with a sweetheart neckline and hellacious knockers swelling out of a nest of midnight lace.

"Look what the Devil and Tom Walker just drug up from the land of Nod," she said to the bartender. "Pour him another whiskey, poor thing. Demon rum for the angel from the underworld. He can't go home yet anyways, it's raining devils and pitchforks out there. He couldn't find the gates of Hell in that downpour, never mind his goddamn car."

The bartender handed me a whiskey and the bill.

"Hell all Friday!" I cried. "Whose bill is this?"

"Lucifer's barber and his three-headed dog," said the bartender. "Who the Devil and Tommy do you think it belongs to? This place was hellful of the Devil and John

Barleycorn and everybody else running drinks on your tab, and you were passed out and off harrowing Hades for all I could rouse out of ya."

"You slept through a real snake-killing mess of Hell eating rats with the Devil's pitchfork," said Wilma. "Two hellpukes come in here carrying sawed-off pool cues looking for some of that devil's dandruff to pack up the old nose. Next thing you know, the cops come in right behind them, hell thrashing alligators, and the biker boys in the back room scattered from hell-to-breakfast."

The bartender leaned into my face. "You was out cold, married to the Devil's daughter, and living with the in-laws. Them cops come in here like hell beating tan bark and the junkies out back went hell-bent for Sunday."

"Those pigs come through here like hell on stilts," said Wilma, "and the gamblers at the tables took off to Hell and gone."

"I'll be goddamned and go-to-helled," says I. "And I slept through the whole durn thing?"

"The archangel Gabriel blowing hornfuls of damnification couldn't'a woke you up," said the bartender. "That's sixty-six dollars and sixty-six cents."

"Hell's banjo!" quoth I. "I ain't paying it."

"The hell you ain't," said the bartender. "You pay it, or I'll go get Satan himself to fuck you up proper. You don't pay I'll knock hell and spots off of you!"

"Hell's peekhole! Ain't you got sixty-six dollars?" asked Wilma, wagging a chest at me that took up Hell and half of Georgia. "I got the Devil's luck and my own too if I'm going home with some lost soul who don't even have sixty-six dollars to his name. I'll lead apes in Hell before I find a man with any cash."

The bartender got to looking like the Devil in Hell, and Wilma got to looking like the deep blue sea and high water.

"Seems I got hell to pay and no pitch hot," says I. "The Devil's dancing in my pockets and there's nothing in his way. I don't suppose you'd take . . ."

"I'd raise merry hell and slip a shingle under it 'fore I'd take a goddamn check," said the barkeep. "Somethin' tells me a check from you ain't worth hell room in Haiti."

"Well," Wilma says, "there's more than one way to whip the Devil 'round the stump."

She battered her eyelashes at the bartender and smiled till Hell wouldn't have it.

"Listen up, hellpup," she says to me, "why don't you fetch your car up front while I find a way to settle up with this horny devil."

No sooner did I get out the front door when, up jumped the Devil, Wilma blew by me like hell on wheels.

"Bolt!!!" she hollered. "Saddle up, Beelzebub, there's hellhounds and notable imps of the Devil coming hell-for-leather right behind us."

Once we got in the car and away from Legion and his diabolic crew, I said, "Hell's fire, Wilma. Where to now?"

"Your place," she said. "It's time to put the Devil into Hell."

"Time to what?" I asked.

"Time to slip in Daintie Davie," Wilma said. "Time to

get Jack in the orchard. Time to feed the dumb glutton. I'm ready to take old Nebuchadnezzar out to grass. My grandmother did it before me, and she called it getting hulled between wind and water. I've got standing room for one. Are you ready to do the divine work of fatherhood, goddamnit?"

"The hell you say," quoth I.

Transfiguration

Money doesn't talk, it swears.

—Bob Dylan, "It's Alright, Ma (I'm Only Bleeding)"

If *fuck you* is primarily a manifestation of male, anal aggression, and *hell* is a display of unconscious stygiophobia (fear of damnation), what makes *shit* such a handy epithet? Or "barnyard epithet," as *The New York Times* would say, because to this day it will not print the word. Out here in the Midwest, we are accustomed to barnyards and it's no big deal to say *shit*, but the *Omaha World Herald* won't print the word either, even though nine-tenths of Nebraska is farmland covered with it.

We may say "Shit!" when we step in shit or open the diaper to receive the latest bequest from the baby, but we don't want to open a newspaper and see four harmless letters typed in a particular sequence. The only possible explanation for this aversion to seeing the word formally printed is that *shit* arouses that fearful thrill, or Freud's sacred fear, we spoke of earlier. "Wagner's music is better than it sounds," Twain once said. And *shit* in print means something more than excrement, more than a barnyard epithet, more than an expletive, which vanishes in an instant along with the gas we use to expel it from our throats. Printed *shit* means too much.

The Library of Congress classification system does not provide a section for books on *shit*, or for books on swearing or dirty words. A researcher wanting to know about *shit* must travel to the BF of psychoanalysis, the PE of slang, the GT of anthropology, the P of literature and literary theory, the N of art, the RC of medical psychiatry, and back to the B of religion and philosophy. Proof positive that *shit* is inextricably bound up with almost everything—creativity, narcissism, money, sex, death, spiritual transformation, autoeroticism—including an array of polarities: rebellion and obedience, aggression and passivity, order and chaos, birth and rebirth, food and waste, hygiene and filth, self-control and dissipation, to name but a few. At least some of these pairings derive from the inherent tension present in any function of the body subject to both voluntary and autonomic control (free will versus determinism, nature versus nurture).

But *shit* also suggests its opposite, food, just as the mouth brings to mind the orifice at the other end of a long, anfractuous passage of secret places where mysterious transformations occur. Most people don't want to think their mouths have anything to do with their assholes, but mouths and assholes, bowels and esophagi have something in common. Even medical science places both openings under the single specialty of gastroenterology, whose practitioners are responsible for inserting endoscopes into mouths and rectums and viewing the intestines or the esophagus, or both. But mouths and assholes have more in common than oppositional locations and functions.

We acquire desirable matter through the mouth, and we dispel the undesirable through an orifice some of us have never laid eyes on. Last night's sumptuous banquet of devoured shapes and textures, the bouquet of colors, flavors, and odors, comes forth the next morning, a single color, a single odor, a single texture, arranged in basically the same shapes, differing only in size and sometimes consistency. What once was food—polymorphous, varietal, cool and warm, moist and dry, cold and hot, aromatic and elementally pleasing, an occasion for good cheer and human fellowship—is squeezed out the next morning in the chilly solitude of the ceramic throne as shit—unitary and homogenous, 98.6 degrees Fahrenheit throughout, monotonous yet somehow repulsive at the same time, and also (at least in our culture) evil in some ineffable way. It is instantly submerged in water and chilled to stifle the stench, which unconsciously reminds us of death. It's immediately flushed, and we expunge all traces in modern rituals meant to instill purity and order.

When one thinks of evil beings or events, one usually imagines something of considerable complexity and hideous detail, something startling, threatening, and deadly. Only shit seems to be evil without being menacing, dramatic, or lethal. Instead it is bland, unremarkable in shape and color. In many cultures and in many epochs it has been administered as medicine, as seasoning in food, and as an aphrodisiac. Shit has been worshipped, eaten, gathered and sold for a profit, combed into the hair, used as a cosmetic and perfume, employed as an amulet for good luck and as an antidote to disease, or smeared on the body to instill courage and endurance. It has been important in mortuary ceremonies, initiation rites, witchcraft, religious ceremonies, hunting, and fishing. Anyone doubting these incongruous uses for shit need only consult John G. Bourke's *Scatologic Rites of All Nations,* a five-hundred-page tome published in 1891 on the history of shit and piss and the rituals surrounding them, with chapter headings such as "The Ordure of the Grand Lama of Thibet" and "Excrement Gods of Romans and Egyptians."

In our more "civilized" societies, shit has become progressively more disreputable as the centuries have passed, despite the efforts of Freud and others. However, shit is currently enjoying a renaissance, at least in the scholarly journals, where Ph.D.s do armchair psychoanalysis on Jonathan Swift's intense disappointment in discovering that the angelic creature he'd selected as his girlfriend actually had bowel movements, and on the relentless shitting of the Yahoos in part four of *Gulliver's Travels.* The Marquis de Sade's works offer the thrill-deprived professor a legitimate excuse for burning the midnight oil over the well-established relationship between shit and sex. James Joyce wrote a few lurid paeans to his wife on the joys of anal intercourse and these, together with Bloom's reveries in the privy in *Ulysses,* provide fodder aplenty for scholarly meditations about shit and why it is so important to literature and the psyche.

Rabelais is another favorite. Literary types use the adjective "Rabelaisian" as a left-handed compliment to an author whose writing is smutty or vulgar. But the sixteenth-century French humanist, physician, and scholar François Rabelais (another dirty-word hero) was more than a smutty writer. In the translator's introduction to the Penguin edition of *Gargantua and Pantagruel,* J. M. Cohen offered this description of Rabelais, and in the process described a state of grace to which many a vulgarian might aspire:

> He was a man intoxicated by every sort of learning and theory, who had at the same time the earthy commonsense of a peasant. His mind would reach out in pursuit of the wildest fancies, and when he had captured them he would relate them only to the three constants of this life: birth, copulation, and death, which he saw in their crudest physical terms. There was in the mind of this loose-living monk no twentieth-century conflict between the two sides of his nature, the scholar's and the peasant's. They played into one another's hands. Nor was he conscious of any inconsistency between his professed beliefs and the often pagan workings of

> his imagination. François Rabelais was a whole
> figure, chock-full of human contradictions,
> which he attempted neither to reconcile nor to
> apologize for.

His books were banned and he was repeatedly forced into hiding, but he remained a relentless optimist with a bottomless faith in the goodness of human nature. His last words were "I owe much; I have nothing; the rest I leave to the poor."

Rabelais understood better than anyone that human beings are most dangerous not when they are being crude or indulging their basest instincts, but when they adamantly insist that they have no base instincts. (Would you feel safer going to a tavern with Falstaff and Jackie Gleason, or to an inquisition and witch burning with Torquemada and Cotton Mather?) As Rabelais observed (by reversing a popular maxim of his age), "If it weren't for the beasts we should all live like scholars."

One of Rabelais's characters, Gargantua, was, at the tender age of five, negotiating the outer limits of what Freud and his followers would later call the anal stage. Rabelais tells us that, after being away at war, Gargantua's father returned and asked the governesses whether "they had kept him sweet and clean."

Gargantua replied that he had already taken care of these matters himself and "that there was not a cleaner boy in all the land." In a parody of scientific shit research, Gargantua described his long, thorough, and earnest search for the very best method for wiping his arse. He had tried wiping himself with a lady's velvet mask, a lady's hood, a lady's neckerchief, some earmuffs of crimson satin, a page's bonnet (all feathered in the Swiss fashion), a March-born cat, and his mother's gloves. He had wiped with sage, fennel, anise, marjoram, roses, gourd leaves, cabbage, beets, vineshoots, marshmallow, lettuce and spinach leaves. He'd tried using his codpiece, the sheets, the coverlet, the curtains, a cushion, a pillow, a slipper, a basket, a lawyer's bag, a penitent's hood, a coif, a hen, a cock, and a hare.

Finally, Gargantua pronounced the results of his grand experiment: "I say and maintain that there is no arse-wiper like a well-downed goose."

Type the search terms *Rabelais* and *excrement* or *ordure* or *scatologic* into one of those computers you find in the reference section of university libraries and you'll get a list of articles written by very well-educated people telling you what all of this means. Readers of Rabelais already know the answer to that question: It's fun!

We would rather read *On the Dignity of Codpieces* than an analysis of the same. We want the good shit, the straight poop, and we have the same aversion to bullshit and bombast that Rabelais identified in describing Gargantua's codpiece: "Not only was it long and capacious, but well furnished within and well victualled, having no resemblance to the fraudulent codpieces of so many young gentlemen which contain nothing but wind, to the great disappointment of the female sex."

According to the word experts, *shit* has been with us

much longer than *fuck,* with a history going back to Old English and beyond. Shit is the greater leveler of human beings, the lowest common denominator, the basest metal in the alchemy of human activity. Saints and sages may fulfill their vows of chastity, but no living person can take a vow of permanent continence; at best they may aspire to regularity.

Because shitting is the most basic act we have in common this side of death, it is the preferred weapon of satirists from Aristophanes to Rabelais and Swift, to Joyce and Pynchon. Bringing shit into any official or formal setting immediately exposes the hypocrisy of popes and presidents and makes them one with pariahs and peasants.

For almost six centuries, beginning in about the tenth, the Catholic Church had a special ceremony for popes, which helps explain the origin of the phrase "seated on the throne" and illustrates how shit is a potent antidote to grandeur. On the new pope's consecration day, a stercoraceous chair (from the Latin *stercus,* for excrement)—a sort of imperial, portable potty—was placed before the door to the basilica. Soon after the new pope was raised on the canopied throne and consecrated, any budding arrogance of office was promptly dispelled by having the pontiff sit on the stercoraceous chair, a reminder of his humanity and an exercise in enforced humility. In the modern ceremony, the procession pauses while attendants burn handfuls of straw, throwing the ashes in the new pope's path, while someone intones, *"Sic transit gloria mundi"* ("Thus passes the glory of the world"). Ask your analyst if black ashes have anything to do with shit. Ask your modern Catholic about the black ashes they smear on their foreheads for Ash Wednesday, a powerful and prominent reminder of shit, death, and dust.

Shit is so fundamental it even animates the roots of the words used to describe it. *Fundament* means "foundation" or "basic principle," but it also means "buttocks" and "anus," as well as "the part of a land surface not altered by human activity." And shitting is a fundament of human nature, a part not altered by all of our "higher" endeavors. Shit's passage through the bowels is a metaphor for the journey of the soul through life. Indeed, one of St. Augustine's immortal lines, *"Inter urinas et faeces nascimur"* (We are born among urine and feces), became a mantra of sorts for Freud and his followers, who quoted it at least once in every volume on psychoanalysis. Shit is the thing itself, dust and ashes. *People* magazine may be featuring you as one of the seventy-two most intriguing or attractive people of the last day and a half, but you may well be reading about it, alone, in a small, quiet room. You'll savor the photo they've taken of you, not noticing the vaguely antiseptic fragrance of the room, designed to mask the other odor, which might cause you to anticipate what you will smell like when you are dead. The mirror will be placed in such a way that you'll see yourself only after you've finished, taken a shower, and are ready to brush your teeth and shave.

A central tenet of Freud's theories of anal eroticism is that our aversion to shit is learned and not instinctual. Shitting is pure, aimless bliss, until our parents intervene with their own hostile opinions—disgust breaking out all over their faces, interrupting what was for us an aromatic and pleasurable experience. But toddlers learn anal aggression, too. As William Gass observed, "Childhood is a civil war." And the first volley is a salvo of shit splattered all over the kitchen floor. Norman O. Brown summed it up best in *Life Against Death: The Psychoanalytic Meaning of History:*

> This infantile stage of anal erotism takes the essential form of attaching symbolic meaning to the anal product. As a result of these symbolic equations the anal product acquires for the child the significance of being his own child or creation, which he may use either to obtain narcissistic pleasure in play, or to obtain love from another (feces as gift), or to assert independence from another (feces as property), or to commit aggression against another (feces as weapon). Thus some of the most important categories of social behavior (play, gift, property, weapon) originate in the anal stage of infantile sexuality and—what is more important—never lose their connection with it.

Freud's ideas about anal aggression may have been indelibly influenced by one of his most famous patients, known as the Wolf Man. In the first therapy session, the Wolf Man offered to have anal intercourse with Freud and shit on his head. Freud apparently never got over it, for as we know, anality is everywhere in psychoanalysis, including within the word itself where -*anal*- forms the torso for *psycho*- and -*ysis*. It's enough to make you wince with irony when psychoanalysts find anality in everything from pipe smoking to orderliness to aggression and parsimony, and then accuse others of being anal.

There is no lack of writers and artists who shockingly or comically have employed descriptions and representations of shit to express rebellion, disdain for pomposity, and even aspirations to metaphysics, but the Italian artist Piero Manzoni probably captured more of shit's subtle, unconscious nuances than any other genius in this field.

In May 1961, Manzoni took ninety tin cans (which look suspiciously like tuna cans) and packed them with his own shit. This was no haphazard undertaking. Manzoni was very precise, exacting, and orderly—some would say anal—in measuring, placing, and sealing exactly thirty grams of his own shit into each can, then labeling each with the following message printed in English, Italian, French, and German:

ARTIST'S SHIT
CONTENTS 30 GRAMS NET
FRESHLY PRESERVED
PRODUCED AND TINNED
IN MAY 1961

Manzoni signed the lid of each can under the words "PRODUCED BY," and each was stenciled with a number, much like a check or a lithograph, showing its place in the series.

The "works" were exhibited in August 1961, with instructions that they be sold by weight based on the price of gold current at the time of sale. Photos of Manzoni, apparently taken to document the making of his art, show a balding cherub with an impish grin standing in a tiled bathroom with a commode plainly visible in the background. Beaming with artistic pride and the creator's delight (or the defecator's relief), Manzoni displays a tin of *Merda d'artista,* holding it out to the camera like a pitchman from a television spot.

Shit and piss have taken on such importance to the art world that an entire issue of *Art Journal* was devoted to scatological works in the fall of 1993, including an essay by Gerald Silk, "Myths and Meanings in Manzoni's *Merda d'artista.*" Silk describes the work as a "transubstantiation of defecation into the gold of art"—a single, bold stroke contrasting and identifying the most precious substance known to man with the most useless, which, according to Silk, suggests alchemy, magic, shamanism, commodity fetishism, and the relationships between process and product in the art world. And that's *before* he gets to Freud and *Merda d'artista*'s obvious debts to the father of psychoanalysis.

In Martin Pops's amazing essay "The Metamorphosis of Shit" (published in *Salmagundi,* 1982), Manzoni's shit containers prompted the author to observe, "It will not do to force this attractive container, to assert the anal priority beneath the sublimations of parsimony and orderliness. The wit of this work lies in its graciousness, the obliquity of its invitation to eat shit."

Transfiguration

Writers are especially anal, because their creations sully white pages with black matter. According to the prominent psychoanalyst Ernest Jones, printed matter is a "curious symbol of feces ... presumably through the association with paper and the idea of pressing (smearing, imprinting)." In former centuries, writers blackened their fingers with the labors of their craft. No need to belabor the link between shit and ink—not only is it black or midnight blue, but it's used to capture emissions of the mouth. This may explain the craving for reading matter one experiences while shitting: we want to read some "shit" to replace the shit we are getting rid of, the bathroom equivalent of getting and spending. In *Memoirs of Martinus Scriblerus,* Alexander Pope describes the birth of a great author:

> Nor was the birth of this great man unattended with prodigies: he himself has often told me, that on the night before he was born, Mrs. Scriblerus dreamed she was brought to bed of a huge ink-horn, out of which issued several large streams of ink, as it had been a fountain. This dream was by her husband thought to signify that the child should prove a very voluminous writer.

Norman Brown attributes the inspiration to Swift, and observes that "even the uninitiated will recognize the fantasy, discovered by psychoanalysis of anal birth."

But Manzoni went beyond infantile playfulness, creativity, and words to capture shit's profoundly serious associations with money. As the infant's first piece of property and first "gift," shit is also an important precursor of cash. Most analysts believe, as does Norman Brown, that "the category of property is not simply transferred from feces to money; on the contrary, money is feces, because the anal eroticism continues in the unconscious." More than a mere symbol, in the human unconscious, money *is* shit. Thomas Pynchon describes Slothrop's New England ancestors in *Gravity's Rainbow* and brings shit, money, and words together in a single revery: "[P]aper—toilet paper, banknote stock, newsprint—a medium or ground for shit, money, and the Word. . . . Shit, money, and the Word, the three American truths."

At the other end of life, shit again assumes paramount importance in the elderly and their obsessions with moving their bowels. Spiritual matters are equally important at the same time in life, and my theory is that the inordinate emphasis the aging citizen places on his bowels occurs when wisdom, long life, and approaching death all conspire to illustrate the fundamental importance of shit.

Getting past our learned attitudes and early programming, which—let's face it!—we acquired solely to appease Mom's militant distaste for washing tubs of diapers and her ritual obsessions with cleanliness and order, we realize that shit is much more than dirty. The process and the product are metaphors for transformation, spiritual as well as physical. As Martin Pops pointed out, "shitting is the bodily archetype of spiritual rebirth insofar as it liberates the body from itself."

Transfiguration

In van Gogh's letters, he often observed that the reek of shit coming from a barn or a fertile field "teaches people something," namely that death and decay are inseparably bound up with life and growth. As Pops tells us:

> All agricultural communities subscribe to the Chinese proverb "waste is treasure," in which the least valued is the most valued: in this equation, shit is death which gives life, the last which shall be first. Shit carries a very powerful double charge, positive and negative, and that is why it is the body's most magical substance.

As with money, to the unconscious, shit not only reminds us of death, it *is* death. Pynchon, the master shit lyricist, again:

> Well there's one place where Shit 'n' Shinola do come together, and that's in the men's toilet at the Roseland Ballroom.... Shit, now, is the color white folks are afraid of. Shit is the presence of death, not some abstract-arty character with a scythe but the stiff and rotting corpse itself inside the whiteman's warm and private own *asshole,* which is getting pretty intimate. That's what that white toilet's for. You see many brown toilets? Nope, toilet's the color of gravestones, classical columns of mausoleums, that white porcelain's the very emblem of Odorless

and Official Death. Shinola shoeshine polish
happens to be the color of Shit. [*Gravity's Rainbow*]

Humans transform matter in the same way black holes
consume light or the way Satan devours sinners and shits
damned souls in those medieval paintings. In many West
African secret societies, young men receive tribal markings
on their torso during their initiations. These marks are
made by the "teeth" of a spirit or devil, who swallows young
boys, digests them, and later discharges them back to the
village as warriors and men.

The gullet's (or the asshole's) intimate association with
transformation in the human unconscious explains much
of the imagery one finds in those popular accounts of near-
death and after-death experiences. These out-of-body
visionaries usually "die" and then are brought back by
modern medical science, because they happen to have qual-
ity health insurance. They return to this world just long
enough to reach their policy limits and spend the money
they make publishing best-selling accounts of their experiences. The imagery found in these accounts reeks of scatol-
ogy and eschatology: There are dark passages and tunnels
with lights at the end; great winds are not uncommon; the
beings describe the sensation of being pushed, forced, or
led along the passage to the light. We need only a few
reports of returned souls who saw big teeth or hair in the
light at the portal openings and the metaphors will be complete.

It's even possible to turn yourself into an asshole by quoting from your own book. In *White Man's Grave*, the protagonist peers for the first time into the black hole of an African latrine:

> He realized his psychology professors had been right in asserting that there is some inexorable, subliminal association between shit and death. The interior of the latrine had a sense of place as powerful as any grave or altar. . . . If shit and death had something in common, it was somewhere down that dark hole—an invisible node where scatology intersected with eschatology, where saprophytes gorged on sap, where man met manure, where the human became humus, where brain, bone, and heart were swallowed by the earth and moldered back into minerals and elements.

Probably the most, ahem, fundamental schism in Christianity occurred when Martin Luther had a religious experience while sitting on the toilet in the tower at Wittenberg. Accounts of this episode are legion, and so are the attempts of Lutherans to pretend it never happened, but here it is, in Luther's own words:

> These words "just" and "justice of God" were a thunderbolt in my conscience. They soon struck terror in me who heard them. He is just, there-

> fore He punishes. But once when in this tower I
> was meditating on those words, "the just lives by
> faith," "justice of God," I soon had the thought
> whether we ought to live justified by faith, and
> God's justice ought to be the salvation of every
> believer, and soon my soul was revived. There-
> fore it is God's justice which justifies us and
> saves us. And these words became a sweeter
> message for me. This knowledge the Holy Spirit
> gave me on the privy in the tower.

To make matters worse (or better), Luther suffered from
recurrent bouts of constipation. Luther himself described
an extended period in 1521 when it took him four or
five days of sweaty labor just to move his bowels. In his
letters, he said God had given him this affliction so that
he would "not be without a relic of the cross." He told
his wife, "I'm like a ripe shit and the world's like a
gigantic asshole." Quoting young Luther, Martin Pops
observes:

> It is fitting, then, that Luther suffered his spiri-
> tual enlightenment on a privy. At the crucial
> moment he relinquished the relic of the cross he
> bore, [he] "was altogether born again and . . .
> entered paradise itself through open gates."

Pops maintains that Luther's doctrine is a "metaphysic of
shitting":

> I do not say a doctrine of justification by faith
> occurred to Luther because he was constipated;
> I say his doctrine is a theological analogy of
> bodily dysfunction. Salvation by faith is the
> doctrine of a man who wants to shit but cannot,
> whose will to shit is of no avail, who must sit
> anxiously and perspiringly, in hope that shit will
> come like grace itself, that sweeter message, in
> a breakthrough of unpredictable issuance. We
> shouldn't disregard the bodily predicate of Lu-
> theran dogma.

Lest anyone think that Lutherans were the only believers hung up on shit, there was a heated theological argument among Catholic scholars through much of the ninth century about whether the Eucharist was subject to digestion and excretion after it was consumed. Aztec art prominently features excremental scenes and deities, and shit for them was at least an ambivalent substance, if not divine.

Martin Pops and Norman O. Brown both catalogue Luther's obsessions with shit and the Devil. Luther's descriptions of Satan are distinctly anal: "The Devil does not come in his filthy black colours, but slinks around like a snake, and dresses himself up as pretty as may be." "The Devil fouls and poisons with his venom the pure and true knowledge of Christ." "We live in the Devil's worm-bag. . . . We are nothing but a worm in ordure and filth, with no good or hope left in us."

The Devil as anality and death instinct was not a new

idea, even in Luther's day. In John Ciardi's translation of the *Inferno*, Dante vividly describes the flatterers he encountered in the eighth circle of Hell as "long lines of people in a river of excrement that seemed the overflow of the world's latrines. I saw among the felons of that pit one wraith who might or might not have been tonsured—one could not tell, he was so smeared with shit." In Dis, at the center of Hell, Satan's upside-down anus is Hell's center of gravity, through which Dante and Virgil pass to ascend into Purgatory. In Joyce's *Portrait of the Artist as a Young Man*, Stephen has a nightmare inspired by one of Father Arnall's famous sermons describing the "awful stench" of Hell, and finds himself in a dreamscape polluted by "clots and coils of solid excrement . . . [featuring] goatish creatures with human faces . . . soft language issuing from their lips, their long swishing tails besmeared with stale shit."

For Freud (and for Luther, too), the Devil's intimate association with shit was part and parcel to shit's identification with gold:

> In ancient civilizations, in myths, fairy tales and superstitions, in unconscious thinking, in dreams and in neuroses—money is brought into the most intimate relationship with dirt. We know that the gold which the devil gives his paramours turns into excrement after his departure, and the devil is certainly nothing else than the personification of the repressed unconscious instinctual life. . . . Indeed, even ac-

> cording to ancient Babylonian doctrine gold is
> "the faeces of Hell" ... It is possible that the
> contrast between the most precious substance
> known to men and the most worthless, which
> they reject as waste matter, has led to this spe-
> cific identification of gold with faeces. [Freud,
> *Character and Anal Eroticism,* 1908]

Our budgetary virtues, our habits of getting and spending, our delight in the new tax preparation and financial
software packages, which allow us to track every cent we
retain or expel and let us categorize our acquisitions and
disbursements, the way the irregular senior citizen records
frequency, consistency, size, color, and shape—all are impulses sublimated from our toilet-training days.

"Doctor," complains the discomfited octogenarian, "I
would feel so much better if I could just manage one, thorough movement a day."

I know how this constipated invalid feels, because I
would feel so much better if I could just spend as much as
I need to, no more and no less.

"Money is dirty," we were told in our childhoods. We
must wash our hands after reveling in the collector's instinct, fingering grimy bills, stacking and arranging the
coins in our collection. And yet Dad left every morning in
pursuit of filthy lucre, avidly grasping after something that
would make him need to wash his hands.

It's *shit*'s double charge that makes it such a friendly
epithet. If *fuck* is a warlike word, if it sounds like two stags

banging antlers, then *shit* is a happy and comradely word. Saying "shit" forces the lips into a grin, which explains the popular expression *shit-eating grin,* whose meaning is felt labially in the person who utters it, rather than in the sense of the words, for who would savor the taste of shit? *Shit* is a buddy word, you say it to somebody else who puts their pants on one leg at a time; somebody who doesn't pretend theirs doesn't stink; somebody who doesn't give a shit or stand on ceremony; somebody who has their shit together.

Know your shit, that's my advice. And if you can find something to read that's funnier than shit, or maybe some deep shit, or some heavy shit, or maybe some interesting or otherworldly shit, buy it in hardcover and collect it, arrange it in alphabetical order on your shelves, enter these books in a relational database, access them by title, author, subject, fiction or non, and add a few notable quotes from each, being careful to include any secondary sources and footnotes. Get really anal about it. On Sunday mornings, take the most expensive book into the bathroom with you, one that's printed on acid-free paper and contains really deep, fundamental insights, precious analects, nice, tight aphorisms and epigrams without a stray word, maxims worth retaining, and proverbs worth espousing.

Come Monday, go do some shitwork and earn some money to buy some more books. And, while at work, if you meet some politically correct shitheads who think they are shit on wheels because their shit doesn't stink, if they make you want to shit bricks because they are trying to regulate the shit you put on the page or the shit that comes out of your mouth, you tell them to go shit in their own backyard and leave your shit alone. Tell them they don't know frog shit from pea soup about the human psyche. They don't know sheep shit from cherry seed, or owl shit from putty. Their brains are so full of shit they couldn't pour piss out of a boot with the directions printed on the heel.

When they start telling you to say "face in the moon" instead of "man in the moon," or "all the ruler's people" instead of "all the king's men," or the "Divinity" instead of "God," or "person of color" (which is such a huge improvement on "colored person"), when they hand you a bias-free guide to language and tell you they expect you to use it, and that they will be counting your he's and she's, you need to take dramatic action.

"I smell shit," you should say. "Ladies and gentleman, I am smelling the most overpowering excremental odors that have ever assaulted an olfactory nerve. I mean, this is the rankest compound of fetors that ever offended a civilized nostril. I am smelling shit all over this room! Someone must have plastered poop with a trowel and a bucket in here! Somebody crapped a payload of Limburger cheese in the thunderbox and forgot to flush. I can't see through the stench to read the clock! I don't want to go on about it, but this feculent reek is peeling skin from my face! The odor is acquiring mass and density, it's threatening my airway!

"I've looked under the table twice, and everybody's pants and pantyhose are still on. The only stools I see are the kind you sit on. So, gentle people, I want to know, whence comes this ghastly malodorousness? Not from your mouths, I hope! Not from your incontinent good intentions! Not from these tidy stacks of bias-free language guides you have for me to read!"

Good and Evil

*H*ow about a language consisting entirely of swearwords,
blasphemy, and obscenity? How about a nice, warm pub
with a roaring hearth and a pool table where that's all you
ever hear? How about a throng of jovial fellows with cloven

153

hooves and faun outfits chalking up a few phallic symbols and racking up a set of Satan's ballocks for a game of nine ball? Would they, could they, invent a language consisting only of cuss words? But if cussing is the norm, then where's the requisite deviance? These hale and hearty fellows would have to invent new words to express compassion and sensitivity, piety and kindness, and then perhaps these "good" words would give them a fearful thrill or sacred fear.

Instead, we have good words and bad ones, and the changing standards by which we judge them. Blasphemy and reverence, doggerel and poetry, vulgarity and politeness, good and evil, love and hate are dyads, polarities, like shit and food. Abolish one, and the other goes with it, which tells you something about the current efforts to abolish hate speech, ridicule, and insult.

I consulted more than a dozen dictionaries and collections of famous quotations on the subject of "politeness," and found at least five negative comments about it for every positive one. Thomas Jefferson called politeness "artificial good humor." Samuel Johnson called it "fictitious benevolence." Ambrose Bierce, in his oft-quoted *Devil's Dictionary*, called it "the most acceptable hypocrisy." Nietzsche referred to politeness several times, always negatively. In addition to his belief that it causes dyspepsia (cited earlier), he also called politeness "that roguish and cheerful vice," and later stressed that he did not want "rudeness to be underestimated: it is by far the most humane form of contradiction and, in the midst of effeminacy, one of our foremost virtues."

As Florence King told us earlier, the best way to bottle up anger is to turn men into women—and women into ladies—by nationwide paroxysms of effeminacy. Certain factions in our workplaces and on our college campuses will get no sleep until bad manners are against the law. One could argue on the strength of the authorities set forth above that instead of statutes abolishing ridicule, vulgarity, and insult in the workplace, we should propose a statute banning politeness and civility. But as I hope I have shown, such a law would take down vulgarity with it, for one cannot exist without the other, any more than you can love someone without occasionally swerving across the centerline into hatred.

This mania for politeness and for legislation directed against hate, hate speech, and hate crimes is attempted thought control, an effort to eradicate character traits, human impulses found in our personality and in society at large. Let's make it a federal crime to conduct one's affairs according to small-minded, petty, xenophobic, pig-ignorant stereotypes, misguided notions, and hare-brained schemes, if those pursuits impinge on the equality of rights of the groups you find listed in Subparagraphs A through F. Beliefs —including discriminatory and "hateful" beliefs—are not discrete modules that can be removed or destroyed by regulatory zeal and social policy. The irony, as Jonathan Rauch pointed out in *Harper's*, "In Defense of Prejudice" (May 1995), is that "the purists pursue prejudice in the name of protecting minorities," forgetting how censorship has been used against minorities in the recent past. "In order to bolster minority self-esteem, they suppress minority opinion."

Sublimation is always better than repression, and a personality is not a bundle of fungible sticks; it bears more resemblance to a symphony orchestra under the direction of a guest conductor. This symphony of the personality is populated by certain headstrong factions of performers, instruments in desperate need of tuning, tubas who love the conductor, cellos who hate him, drunk percussionists, frivolous piccolo players, and several Byzantine backstabbers clutching their instruments like smoking daggers and eyeing the spot between the shoulder blades of the First Violin. William Gass describes this cacophony of competing human appetites in an essay called "On Talking to Oneself":

> Plato thought of the soul as an ardent debating society in which our various interests pled their causes; and there were honest speeches and dishonest ones; there was reason, lucid and open and lovely like the nakedness of the gods, where truth found its youngest friend and nobility its ancient eloquence; and there was also pin-eyed fanaticism, deceit and meanness, a coarseness like sand in cold grease; there was bribery and seduction, flattery, browbeating and bombast. Little has changed, in that regard, either in our souls or in society since.

Using modern brain-imaging techniques, researchers are now able to "watch" patterns of magnetic and electrical activity and glucose consumption in the human brain as it thinks. A new breed of brain scientists called cognitive neuroscientists is attempting to understand how the brain gives itself the illusion that we have a single "voice" or "point of view" inside of us, when in fact consciousness consists of a small swamp of neurons firing in specialized networks that converge in no particular arena or center of command. The conclusions of these neurophilosophers sound suspiciously like Plato's and Gass's observations that the human sensibility is a Hydra of competing urges and demands—what early Christians called *psychomachia,* or the warfare of the soul. Quoting neuroscientist Daniel Dennett, author of *Consciousness Explained,* an article in *Newsweek* put it this way:

> Early popular representations often showed a homunculus pushing buttons and pulling levers in the skull. Dennett posits swarms of these figurative imps, a "Pandemonium of Homunculi," all clamoring and competing for attention, like traders on the floor of the stock exchange. Each of them specializes in different aspects of perception—shape, language, motion and so on. As they go about their tasks, they confer with each other and form coalitions, producing "collated, revised, enhanced" drafts of the raw

data they take in. "Information entering the
nervous system is under continuous 'editorial
revision,' so that at any point in time there are
multiple 'drafts' of narrative fragments at various stages of editing in various places in the
brain."

Out of this stream of incoming data from the outside
world and the rioting impulses prompted by our instincts,
our past experiences, our hormones, our nervous systems,
and our metabolisms, we strike a series of balances, an "I"
that is nothing more than a fragile, momentary truce
among competing factions trying to take the floor in the
parliament of consciousness. Some of these interior voices
shout for attention, speak poetry, throw tantrums, sing
arias, swear violently, love exercise, hate broccoli, crave
booze, need sleep, pray eloquently, experiment with drugs,
and urge us to do and say the heroic and the unspeakable.
Some of these internal creatures are tender nightingales
lulling our children to sleep, and others are monstrous basi-
lisks who kill their enemies with a baleful glance.

Even our casual expressions show that we are anything
but unitary creatures: "I'm of two minds about going to
Europe." "Half of me says leave him for good, and the other
half says marry him." "I can't make up my mind" (because
there are too many dissenting voices).

"The brain," insists Marvin Minsky of the Massachusetts
Institute of Technology, is just "hundreds of different ma-

chines . . . connected to each other by bundles of nerve fibers, but not everything is connected to everything else. There isn't any 'you' " (*Newsweek,* April 20, 1992).

The language police believe there is a you and they want to make sure you—and all the components of your personality—behave themselves. No Freudian slips, no dirty jokes. Don't make passes and don't be vulgar. They believe in the Orwellian idea that if you make enough "bad" words illegal, if you draft statutes banning ridicule and insults, and compel the use of "correct" language, pretty soon people will be unable to conceive of harassment and hatred, because they will have no words to formulate or express the ideas. What they really want is a "moral" existence where there are no choices, where one is unable to speak one's mind if one's mind contains hateful thoughts. Make racial invective and gender-based assumptions illegal, the argument goes, and soon people will forget how to think them. Bigots and misogynists will be unable to infect others and instead will take their warped ideas to the grave with them.

Eventually, the consciousness of the entire human race will be raised, and we will return to a state of Noble Sensitivity, oozing concern for one another and celebrating our differences. We will be transported back to the Garden, before Adam ate the apple, before Satan said, "I will not serve!" People will be good by default, because bad language will be eradicated by fiat. God will yawn down from on high, while Man scurries around underfoot trying to think of new ways to please his master.

If you took two human beings, blinded them, deafened them, cut off their limbs, stuffed rags in their mouths, stacked them on top of each other, and kept them alive by intravenous feeding, they eventually would develop a language, probably one based upon the syntax of the nervous system, a sort of palpable dermographia, whereby ideas and emotions would be conveyed tactilely by way of epidermal braille. Instead of sounds traveling in waves through space, instead of the hand shapes and facial expressions of American Sign Language, "words" for these human chunks would reverberate through the skin in the form of grammatical sensations. Or maybe their nerves would simply grow into each other's skins, mesh in some interhuman network, form postlingual Siamese twins. Rest assured, they would communicate, somehow.

Human beings "do" language, Steven Pinker tells us in *The Language Instinct,* the same way that bats do sonar or spiders spin webs. "In nature's talent show we are simply a species of primate with our own act, a knack for communicating information about who did what to whom by modulating the sounds we make when we exhale." Who did what to whom embraces everything from sacrificing your life to save somebody else's to mounting someone against their will because they happened to be holding still and weaker than you. There are as many "good" and "bad" words for these activities as there are people who indulge in or observe them. And Pinker adamantly belittles the impulse of grammarians to tell us that some language structures are inherently "better" than others:

> It is even a bit misleading to call Standard English a "language" and these variations "dialects," as if there were some meaningful difference between them. The best definition comes from the linguist Max Weinreich: a language is a dialect with an army and a navy.

Certain political factions are enlisting the army and navy of the federal courts to enforce their version of politically correct "Standard English." Fortunately the language instinct is much too powerful and versatile to be attacked by anything as cumbersome as a federal bureaucracy. The job of language will be accomplished one way or another, Pinker tells us, and human beings have proven infinitely resourceful when it comes to inventing languages and bending words, gestures, facial expressions, music, colors, and forms to the tasks and pleasures of communication.

In the beginning was the Word, but St. John is understandably more interested in the *logos* and Christology of the expression than in telling us how the spark of language leapt between the first humans and charged them with a divine ability to communicate. The Bible tells us God's first Word was His Son, Jesus Christ, the *logos*. The Bible doesn't tell us about Man's first word. Was it indecent, profane, vulgar, blasphemous, obscene, grammatically correct, prayerful, an elaboration of the cooing of doves or the screeching of howler monkeys? What Pinker attributes to a biological force in human beings could as easily have derived from God's profound loneliness and His wanting someone to talk to. At the instant God touched us, the Word surged through the human community with the force of sap being forced through nature's green fuses of vegetation.

Language, words, cannot be inherently "bad" or "good," any more than people can be inherently "vulgar" or "polite." And any legislation aimed at censoring speech in the name of civil rights should be viewed with the same skepticism with which we now view laws from the last century that forbade something called blasphemy. It's the same game: edit the speech of your ideological opponent by passing laws against the use of specific, offensive words. But good and evil are not simple, guileless creatures. They frequently masquerade in each other's costumes, and like ventriloquists, adopt and throw each other's voices. It is impossible to mount a surgical strike against either one of them by attempting to excise certain words or phrases from the language. Passing laws against saying "Men are better than women" is like trying to abolish certain styles of handwriting, because experts have determined that they indicate a criminal pathology.

The irony of passing laws against blasphemy is that blasphemy proves the existence of God just as surely as does piety; just as surely as vulgarity proves politeness, obscenity proves virtue, and discrimination proves equality. "Blasphemy itself could not survive religion," said G. K. Chesterton; "if anyone doubts that let him try to blaspheme Odin." The Marquis de Sade's first arrest for his notorious escapades occurred after he paid Jeanne Testard, a twenty-year-old fan maker who "met men occasionally," to go with him to an apartment furnished with crucifixes, religious paintings, chalices, and other religious icons. The Marquis began the encounter with a torrent of blasphemy and claimed that he had proved that God does not exist. He wanted the woman to help him defile the holy objects and proposed using them to perform various sexual acts, after which they would go to Holy Mass, take Communion, and make off with two hosts, which they could defile upon returning to his apartment. The terrified woman adamantly refused and fought off the marquis's advances, until she was released the next morning and went straight to the police.

At first blush, the marquis seems a paragon of blasphemy indeed, but upon closer consideration his behavior makes little sense for an atheist. Maurice Lever, the most recent and compelling biographer of Sade, makes the point in *Sade: A Biography:*

> This taste for sacrilege is rather surprising and more than a little odd in a man who throughout his life denied the existence of God. Blasphemy makes sense only as transgression of a recognized value. The true atheist is not the person who combats God by denying that he exists but the one who never thinks about his existence. Such a contradiction raises doubts about the reality of Sade's atheism. The more the Marquis rails against religion (and his hatred of priests was close to hysterical), the less convincing he is.

> Silence on this issue would have been a hundred times more convincing than all his invective. To deny that the host and crucifix are sacred and then choose them as instruments of revolt seems naive.

Sade was the kind of embittered atheist described by Orwell, "the sort of atheist who does not so much disbelieve in God as personally dislike Him." The marquis was a crafty psychologist himself and anticipated this argument in *La Philosophie dans le Boudoir,* published thirty-two years after the episode with Jeanne Testard. Sade argued that "for the atheist sacrilege can be justified if it is a stimulus to pleasure." Lever calls this defense "admittedly shrewd, but it fails to carry conviction, for even if making a fetish of sacred objects excites the senses, it still implies recognition of the sacred as such":

> In regard to religion as to so many other values it seems to me that Donatien de Sade remained a "very young head," capable of spewing forth "horrible impieties" expressly to provoke the wrath of adults, which he found exciting. Religious objects were never a matter of indifference to him (cold contempt was not in his nature). His attitude toward them would continue to be one of impotent rage accompanied by immature gestures of defiance.

Good and Evil

What do the Marquis de Sade and the word police have in common? If human beings are truly equal in the eyes of all but a few warped bigots, then why the poisonous rage against the merest suggestion that some might think they are better than others? Is the truth so anemic that it requires protection from words? And why fear the rancor of chauvinists and bigots? Their opinions are nothing more than the transgression of a recognized value. It's like passing laws banning use of the word *God* because people might use it to say He does not exist.

Blasphemy proves the existence of the Divinity as surely as evil proves good, and the Devil proves God. Norman O. Brown made the same observation in the context of cosmic psychoanalysis: "If we want to understand Luther, we may, if we like, take neither his God nor his Devil seriously, and substitute psychological explanations for both. What we may not do is to take one seriously and explain away the other. For Luther, as for John Wesley, 'No Devil, no God.' "

The obsession with "values," which perennially grips the nation for about a month—the sort of frenzied, short-lived soul-searching you get from a high school retreat—has recently been swallowed up by an obsession with equality. Deep down, the modern citizen who believes first and foremost in civil rights and the equal worth of all can't bring herself or himself to call anyone evil, unless it's a violent white male trying to deprive someone of their equality rights. How can anything or anybody be bad or good if we are all created absolutely equal with an equal right to equal rights, and an absolute right to assert and protect our rights with lots of litigation? People aren't bad or good, they're equal.

Hollywood knows what really sells, though, and it's not equality, it's hatred. It's not enough to make a feel-good movie about women and oppressed minorities achieving self-actualization, discovering their inner children, and obtaining their fair share of equality rights; we're missing a villain. "Here," the entertainment industry says, "don't hate these poor women or those poor colored folk. Hate this insensitive, ignorant, bigoted, white male fuckpig of a sheriff and slave owner. Don't worry, he'll get his before this flick's over. There! Doesn't that hatred feel much better than the hatred you see these bigots using against helpless minorities?"

Justice as a main course is just not filling, unless it's accompanied by a generous dollop of revenge. Nietzsche expressed this notion by borrowing a French word, *ressentiment*. It's not enough for us to discover the truth, to discern the equality of all people, or to live a righteous life, we also need to attack everyone who happens to hold a contrary view. We are insecure in our beliefs, as long as there are other people walking around smiling and equally convinced of a contrary notion. We not only want to convert them, we also want to punish them.

This is a common feature of zealotry and of most ideologies, not just political correctness and multiculturalism, but also Nazism, reactionary Catholicism, born-again Christianity, pro-life activists, pro-abortion activists, and the

National Rifle Association. Compromise is unthinkable, because it would dilute Truth. As one reviewer pointed out in *The New Yorker,* "The central paradox of political correctness is that it demands diversity in everything except thought."

But when ideology marries power, that's when the real entertainment known as retribution begins. Listen to St. Thomas Aquinas assuring medieval Christians that their rewards in Heaven will consist of a lot more than simple truths and heavenly bliss:

> In order that the bliss of the saints may be more delightful for them and that they may render more copious thanks to God for it, it is given to them to see perfectly the punishment of the damned. [*Summa Theologiae,* III, Supplementum, Q. 94, Article 1]

And in order that the bliss of the equal shall be more delightful for them, it is given to them to see perfectly civil litigation, criminal prosecution, and public humiliation of bigots and sexual harassers. At the beginning of the *Inferno,* Dante is filled with compassion at the sight of so many suffering so much in Hell. Early on, Virgil even upbraids him and warns him not to take pity on those whom God has seen fit to punish. A few cantos later, old Dante is merrily stepping on the heads of sinners in raptures of self-righteous anger.

Equal pay for equal work, equal job opportunities, equal

job responsibilities are not enough, we still need to punish the guy who tells dirty jokes and thinks women don't make good doctors. Should anyone be surprised to discover that professions and workplaces dominated by women are rife with the same abusiveness, harassment, ridicule, and stereotypical insults directed against men? Ask a male nurse, or an employee of Jenny Craig or any other "female-dominated" corporation. Does anyone doubt that pro-lifers (who profess to believe in the sanctity of human life) would fill a stadium if they knew they could feed a few abortion-rights activists to the lions? Or that abortion proponents (who believe in choice for everybody except pro-lifers) would throng the town square to see a few clinic picketers drawn and quartered?

The last place the virtuous ideologue looks for evil is in his own heart. "It is among people who think no evil," observed Logan Pearsall Smith, "that Evil can flourish without fear." As long as we use the correct terminology to describe the disadvantaged and the differently abled, as long as we are deferential to the beliefs and ideologies of everyone except bigoted white males, there is no reason to suspect ourselves of evil. Evil lives in the hearts of biased people who use "bad" words and discriminate against others.

It's the same mysterious solace we take in movies about the Holocaust. We have identified true evil, found a receptacle where it can be displaced and confined. There is no need to fear that it may still be on the loose out there, or—God

forfend—in here with me. It's out there and back in time.
It's those Nazis, not me.

We want to think of everyone as equal and good, but it's
just too much fun to hate "evil" people, whereupon snakes
promptly hatch in our own bosoms. We hate them, we can't
wait to punish them, but we also want to know more about
them, how they came by their warped beliefs, and why they
behave so terribly. We are curious about how evil works,
if for no other reason than that it provides contrast and
background to virtue. Is evil a formative influence, in the
same way that a mordant is used for etching? Why is it that
Dante's *Divine Comedy* consists of three books—*Inferno*,
Purgatorio, and *Paradiso*—and the only one people read is
the *Inferno*?

Roget's International Thesaurus contains at least twice as
many synonyms for *bad person* as it does for *good person*.
They appear side by side in the volume, and if you read
them as guest lists to two different dinner parties, or as a
cast list from two different plays, the discrepancy in popularity is manifest.

Do you want to spend the evening sampling the dialogue
and observing the behaviors of *good egg, stout fellow, salt of
the earth*, and *pillar of society*? Or would you rather go
downstairs and watch the person Shakespeare called a *base,
proud, shallow, beggarly, three-suited, hundred-pound, filthy,
worsted-stocking knave*?

Do you want to see *gentleman and a scholar* meet *Mr.
Nice Guy* for a nonalcoholic beer and baked Tostitos at *good*

Joe's place? Or would you prefer going to the Bad Person Theater, so you can see what happens when *ne'er-do-well, wastrel, scoundrel, reprobate, miscreant, motherfucker, swine, skunk, polecat, culprit, swindler, desperado, jailbird, scum of the earth, jackdaw of Belial,* and *imp of Satan* are all thrown into the same lockup at two A.M. in Hell's Kitchen?

Shakespeare waxes eloquent no matter what the moral flavor of the character at hand, but the sheer genius and invention of calling someone an "elvish-marked abortive rooting hog," a "slave of nature and the son of hell," a "slander of thy heavy mother's womb," surpasses the poetry of telling your best friend you'll wear him in your heart of hearts. That's why Richard III is the lead, and Horatio, Hamlet's buddy, is a stage prop, a straight man for the prince's haunted, terminal inability to do anything.

It's literary proof of Oscar Wilde's observation that "it is absurd to divide people into good and bad. People are either charming or tedious." Hugh Rawson quotes the Reverend Richard Chnevix Trench, a nineteenth-century philologist and divine, who said, "[I]t is a melancholy thing to observe how much richer is every vocabulary in words that set forth sins, than in those that set forth graces. . . . How much wit, yea, how much imagination must have stood in the service of sin, before it could possess a nomenclature so rich, so varied, and often so heaven-defying as it has."

Flannery O'Connor was once asked by a group of nuns to help edit a manuscript about a gifted child disfigured by cancer, who died as a result of the disease at the age of twelve. In the process of wrestling with the usual mysterious collisions of good and evil, O'Connor made the same complaint about the prolixity of testaments to evil, but added that the dearth of tributes to "good" may be because good can also be "grotesque":

> This opened up for me . . . a new perspective on the grotesque. Most of us have learned to be dispassionate about evil, to look it in the face and find, as often as not, our own grinning reflections with which we do not argue, but good is another matter. Few have stared at that long enough to accept the fact that its face too is grotesque, that in us the good is something under construction. The modes of evil usually receive worthy expression. The modes of good have to be satisfied with a cliché or a smoothing down that will soften their real look. ["A Memoir of Mary Ann," in *Mystery and Manners*]

It's too bad Flannery O'Connor died young and before the invention of political correctness, because she had an unerring eye for the smugness of "virtuous" people. Her favorite character was the sort of deadly earnest purist whom you find sitting on those student tribunals holding inquisitions meant to enforce campus speech codes—somebody who has been possessed of the truth since adolescence and spends the rest of their life tsk-tsking, shaking their head, and waging war against the follies of evil and ignorance—occasionally stooping to attempt reform. These people are so impatient they don't have time for a concept of "good under construction," or good as a balance of competing and sublimated forces, they want "good" now, the finished product, and they want it required by law. Of course, humorless zealots rarely recognize themselves and their "grotesque" virtues, unless it happens to be in an apocalyptic vision on the order of the one O'Connor describes at the end of a story called "Revelation":

> There was only a purple streak in the sky, cutting through a field of crimson and leading, like . . . a vast swinging bridge extending upward from the earth through a field of living fire. Upon it a vast horde of souls were rumbling toward heaven. There were whole companies of white-trash, clean for the first time in their lives, and bands of black niggers in white robes, and battalions of freaks and lunatics shouting and clapping and leaping like frogs. And bringing up the end of the procession was a tribe of people whom she recognized at once as those who, like herself and Claud, had always had a little of everything and the God-given wit to use it right. She leaned forward to observe them closer. They were marching behind the others with great dignity, accountable as they had always been for good order and common sense and respectable behavior. They alone were on key. Yet she could

see by their shocked and altered faces that even their virtues were being burned away.

Unless they have omitted the works of dead white males from their curricula, English literature professors perennially are forced to remark on the attraction of evil in Milton's *Paradise Lost,* in which the most interesting character is Lucifer, beside whom all the virtuous angels seem two-dimensional figurines by comparison. It's not an easy thing to explain. We can be facile about it, like Oscar Wilde, who said, "I like persons better than principles, and I like persons with no principles better than anything else in the world." We can be cute, like Mae West: "Between two evils, I always pick the one I never tried before," or, "When I'm good, I'm very, very good, but when I'm bad, I'm better." But a quick wit is no substitute for profundity.

We want to know more about why Lucifer would rather rule Hell than serve Heaven. Milton seduces us and puts us inside the Devil's head, the same way a certain part of us privately empathizes with Shakespeare's best villains. Isn't the enforced virtue of Heaven a kind of slavery? Conversely, Hell, though a miserable place, at least offers the possibility of freedom from the tyranny of the Creator. Doesn't it? Who wants to be second fiddle for all eternity? Satan's struggle is our struggle, and we want to know just how he arrived at the wrong decision.

Another, more frightening explanation comes from William Blake, another guy who wrote about the paradoxical double valences of Heaven and Hell: "The reason Milton wrote in fetters when he wrote of Angels & God, and at liberty when of Devils & Hell, is because he was a true Poet and of the Devil's party without knowing it."

This notion that writers, artists, musicians—congenital slaves to paint, sounds, good words and bad ones—are somehow accomplices to evil or limbs of the Devil was once a popular theory. It seemed to Parisian concertgoers in the eighteenth century that the great Paganini never practiced, yet he was the greatest violinist of his day, so most thought he had sold his soul to the Devil in exchange for his talent. The story of Faust trading his soul for perfect knowledge in his pact with Mephistopheles has been told and retold in operas, poems, symphonies, novels, movies—often recast to accommodate the artist's obsession with mastery of form and technique.

Scarier still for the modern author is a passage from one of Kafka's letters:

> But what about this being a writer as such? Writing is a sweet and marvelous reward, but a reward for what? In the course of the night it became clear to me, as plain as a children's show-and-tell lesson, that it is a reward for serving the devil. This descent down to the dark powers, this unleashing of ghosts by nature bound, these questionable embraces and whatever else may be going on down there, none of it remembered as one writes stories in the sun-

light up above. Perhaps there are also different ways of writing, but I only know this one; at night, when fear keeps me from sleeping, I only know this one. [Ernst Pawel, *The Nightmare of Reason: A Life of Franz Kafka*]

The temptation for the modern political animal obsessed with equality is the same. It's the urge Robert Bork described in *The Tempting of America*, namely: At what point do we bargain away the soul of the Constitution and render it meaningless by reading into it every passing, well-intentioned urge of the majority in power? If the Constitution protects something as controversial and as morally questionable as abortion today, what sort of atrocities will it protect when a new majority arrives in the next century? After all, it's the same Constitution that the Supreme Court once used to proclaim that people with black skins are property. Shall we now use it to proclaim that people with biased views are hate criminals?

Hate speech is the product of disordered thinking, therefore we should punish it? Laughter, too, is a dissolution of sorts, but so far no legislation has been proposed to ban it. Perhaps it's best to keep quiet about this, because the word police are so deadly earnest in their mission and take themselves so seriously that they would jump at the chance to abolish laughter, beginning with the criminalization of any laughter that takes place at the expense of others.

You laugh? It couldn't happen? It's a short step from banning ridicule and insult in the workplace to making laughter illegal as well. Insult, ridicule, and laughter all are inspired by a sense of one's own superiority, which sounds suspiciously like elitism and a deprivation of equality rights. Listen to Charles Baudelaire tell us about the primordial evil called laughter in his essay "On the Essence of Laughter" (1855):

> [I]t is certain that human laughter is intimately linked with the accident of an ancient Fall, of a debasement both physical and moral. Laughter and grief are expressed by the organs in which the command and the knowledge of good and evil reside—I mean the eyes and the mouth. . . . Laughter comes from the idea of one's *own* superiority. A satanic idea, if there ever was one! . . . Laughter is satanic: it is thus profoundly human . . . [and] essentially contradictory; that is to say that it is at once a token of an infinite grandeur and an infinite misery.

What the Germans called *Schadenfreude*, a malicious delight in the misfortunes of others, is best expressed by—you guessed it—laughter. Therefore, laughter should be banned from the workplace because it is often abusive, creates a hostile environment, and depends for its expression on a sense that one is "better" than others. See how this works?

This is to say nothing of unconscious thought crimes, for a recent series of Supreme Court cases suggests that it doesn't matter if discrimination is unintentional—it can be proved by workforce statistics alone! One could argue that unintentional discrimination is the worst, most virulent kind, precisely because it's so insidious and has its origins in the unconscious.

As Plato observed in *The Republic:*

> Our dreams feed on our repressed longings. The ordinary man only dreams what the criminal carries out . . . part of the soul dares everything, as if it were loose from every shame and every sensibility. It does not hesitate to rape its mother with the imagination, or to give itself to anyone, be it man, god, or animal; no murder draws it back, no nourishment does it abstain from; in short there is no insensible or shameless deed it is not ready to carry out.

Suppose you wanted to discuss such a dream in the workplace. Assuming you are a nonunion employee working in an at-will-employment state, any employer would have the perfect right to fire you for this or for any other reason. But the word police aren't satisfied with trusting the instincts of self-interested employers, who may value an employee's skills and put up with his kinky nightmares. They want federal statutes guaranteeing that women, minorities, elderly people, disabled people, people of various religious persuasions, and whoever else musters the political power to get added to the list will be treated politely and protected from biased speech, insults, and ridicule. And if someone wants to discuss a misogynistic dream, take issue with someone's religion, tell a dirty joke, or express an opinion about menstruation or male insensitivity, they should be sued for punitive damages.

This well-intentioned impulse to censure the vocabulary of hate manifests the same confusion between word and deed, between object and the name describing it that anthropologists of the last century once attributed to "savages." As I hope I have shown, this predilection for creating tabooed words is universal, powerful, and dangerous. But, like other powerful human impulses, it packs a double charge, for it also proves our moral faculty.

If we were beasts of the field and hearth and nothing more, *fuck* would be a sound issuing from the larynx of a rooting sow. No syllable would be more disgusting than any other. If we were uncomplicated, equal, and resolutely virtuous, all words, like all people, would be absolutely equal, none "better" than any other. James Joyce's anal-fantastic letters to his wife would be no more offensive than the deadly dull language of Title VII or any other of the 150,000 pages of federal regulations that allegedly protect us from all manner of "evil."

We are something more than that, thanks to our ability to distinguish good words from bad ones. But does being able to tell them apart mean we should ban the bad ones? *Discriminate* against bad words? Why? If our capacity to take offense depends on dirty words and hateful speech, abolishing them would eradicate not just the words, but our moral perceptions of them, too. If "bad" words are banned, only "good" words remain, and distinctions would vanish along with our ability to perceive them. We would never look for better bread than comes from wheat, nor would we listen for better air in the words we hear; words would simply do their job and we would understand them, or they would be meaningless. Never would we pass judgment on a word except for its utility in expressing what was on its employer's mind at the time he uttered it. And for modern man there seems to be an unfortunate, insistent need for profane, vulgar, blasphemous, hateful speech, because our mental state is overwrought and regressing.

In the final analysis, all of this linguistic foofaraw, all this confusion of good and evil, of hatred for minorities mixed in with hatred of bigots, may go to prove nothing more than that it is easy and fun to hate, the road to Hell is wide and downhill, and the path to Heaven is narrow, ascending, and treacherous. But, as Heracleitus told us long ago, the path up and down are one and the same. If that is true, then the divinity unfairly discriminates against people with evil inclinations. And we could never abide a God who discriminates. Could we?

About the Author

RICHARD DOOLING is a writer and a lawyer specializing in employment discrimination. His second novel, *White Man's Grave,* was a finalist for the National Book Award in fiction. He lives in Omaha, Nebraska, with his wife and children.

About the Type

Minion is a 1990 Adobe Originals typeface by Robert Slimbach. Minion is inspired by classical, old style typefaces of the late Renaissance, a period of elegant, beautiful, and highly readable type designs. Created primarily for text setting, Minion combines the aesthetic and functional qualities that make text type highly readable with the versatility of digital technology.